TRACING
LETTERS

TRACING LETTERS

TRACING LETTERS

TRACING

LETTERS

TRACING LETTERS

TRACING LETTERS

TRACING LETTERS

TRACING LETTERS

TRACING
LETTERS

TRACING LETTERS

TRACING LETTERS

TRACING LETTERS

TRACING LETTERS

TRACING
LETTERS

TRACING LETTERS

TRACING LETTERS

TRACING LETTERS

TRACING
LETTERS

TRACING LETTERS

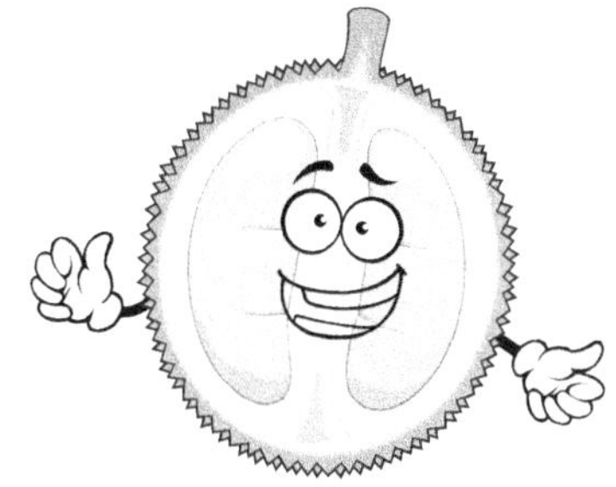

TRACING LETTERS

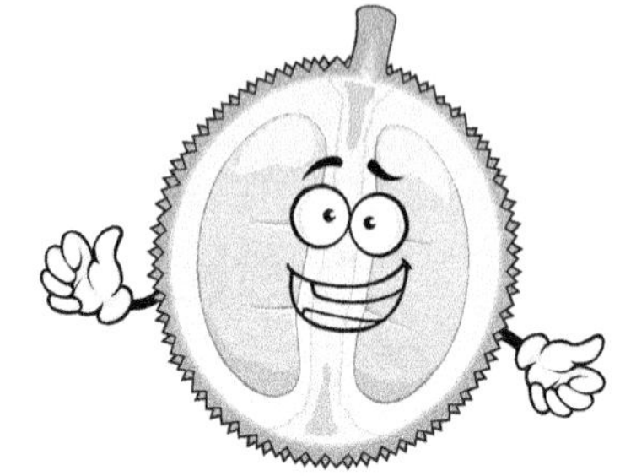

TRACING LETTERS

TRACING LETTERS

TRACING LETTERS

TRACING LETTERS

TRACING LETTERS

TRACING
LETTERS

TRACING LETTERS

TRACING LETTERS

TRACING LETTERS

TRACING
LETTERS

TRACING LETTERS

TRACING
LETTERS

TRACING LETTERS

TRACING LETTERS

TRACING LETTERS

TRACING LETTERS

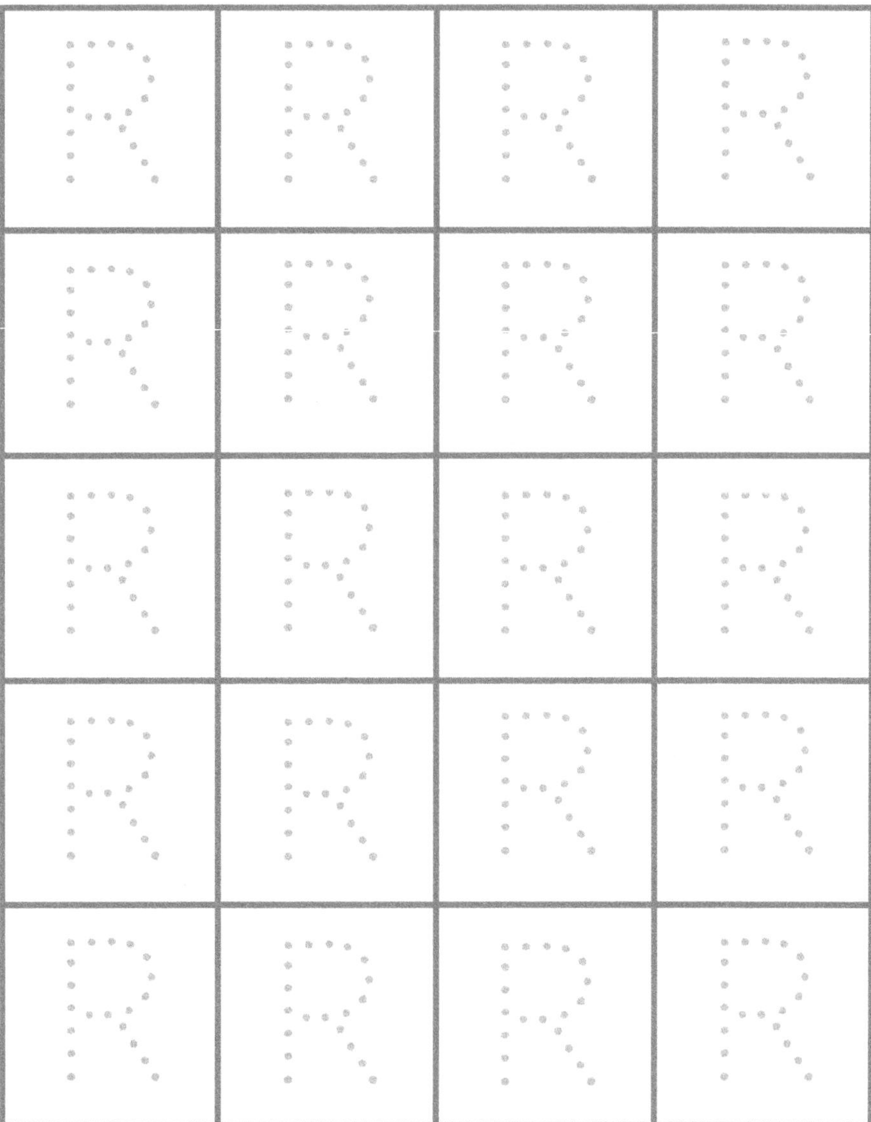

TRACING LETTERS

TRACING LETTERS

TRACING LETTERS

TRACING LETTERS

TRACING LETTERS

TRACING
LETTERS

TRACING LETTERS

TRACING LETTERS

TRACING

LETTERS

TRACING

LETTERS

TRACING LETTERS

TRACING
LETTERS

TRACING LETTERS

TRACING LETTERS

TRACING LETTERS

TRACING LETTERS

UPPERCASE HANDWRITING PRACTICE

A B C D E F G

H I J K L M N

O P Q R S U

U V W X Y Z

UPPERCASE HANDWRITING PRACTICE

A B C D E F G

H I J K L M N

O P Q R S U

U V W X Y Z

DIRECTIONS: TRACE THE WORDS THAT BEGIN WITH THE LETTER A

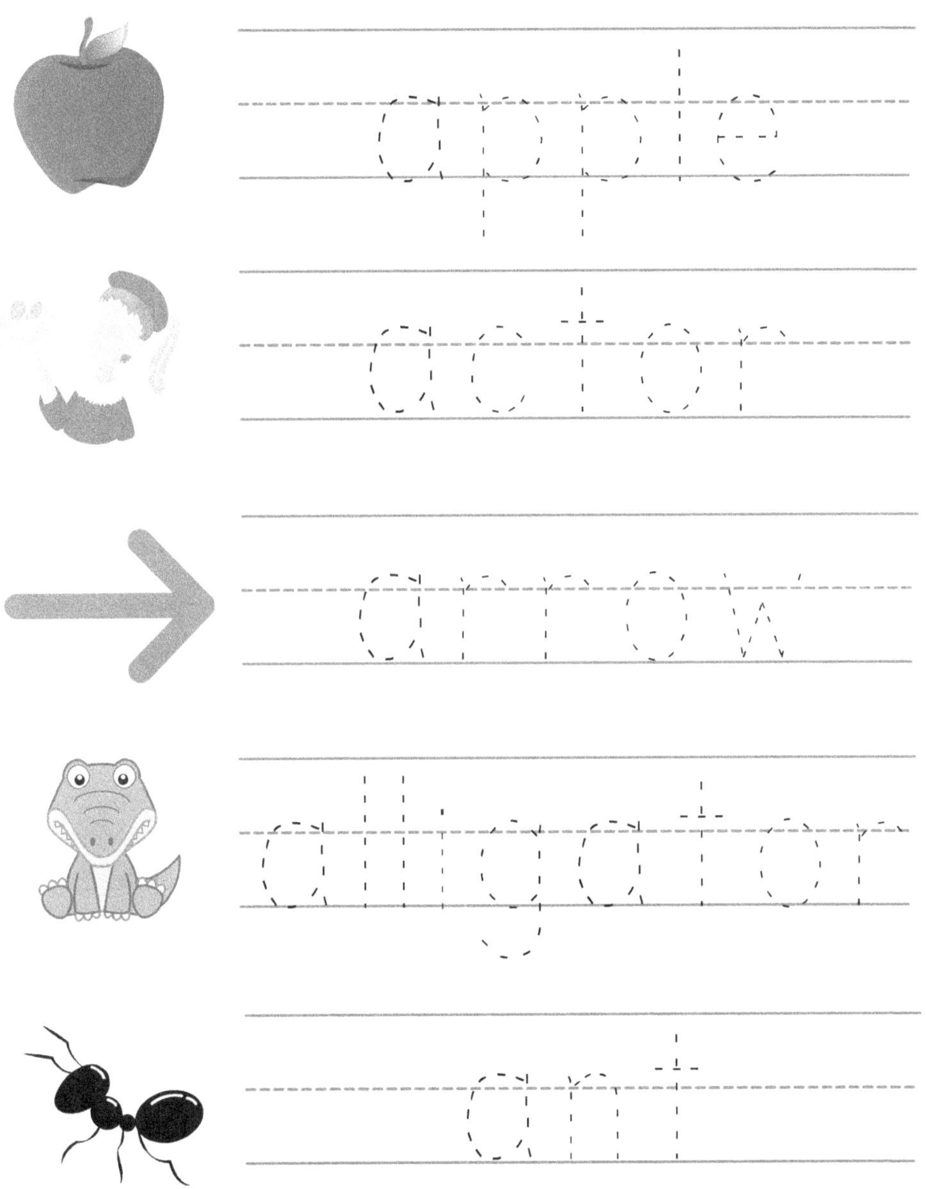

DIRECTIONS: TRACE THE WORDS THAT BEGIN WITH THE LETTER A

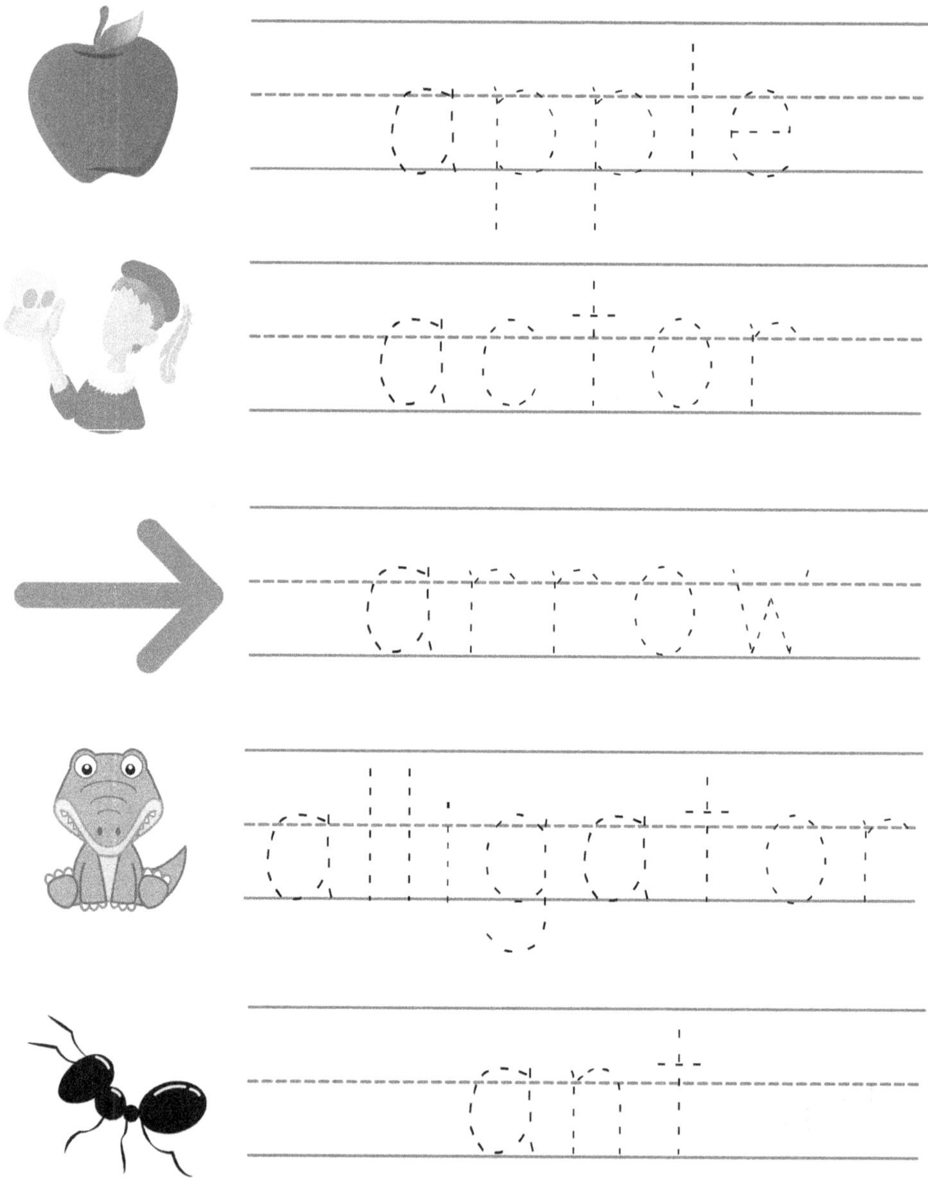

DIRECTIONS: TRACE THE WORDS THAT BEGIN WITH THE LETTER B

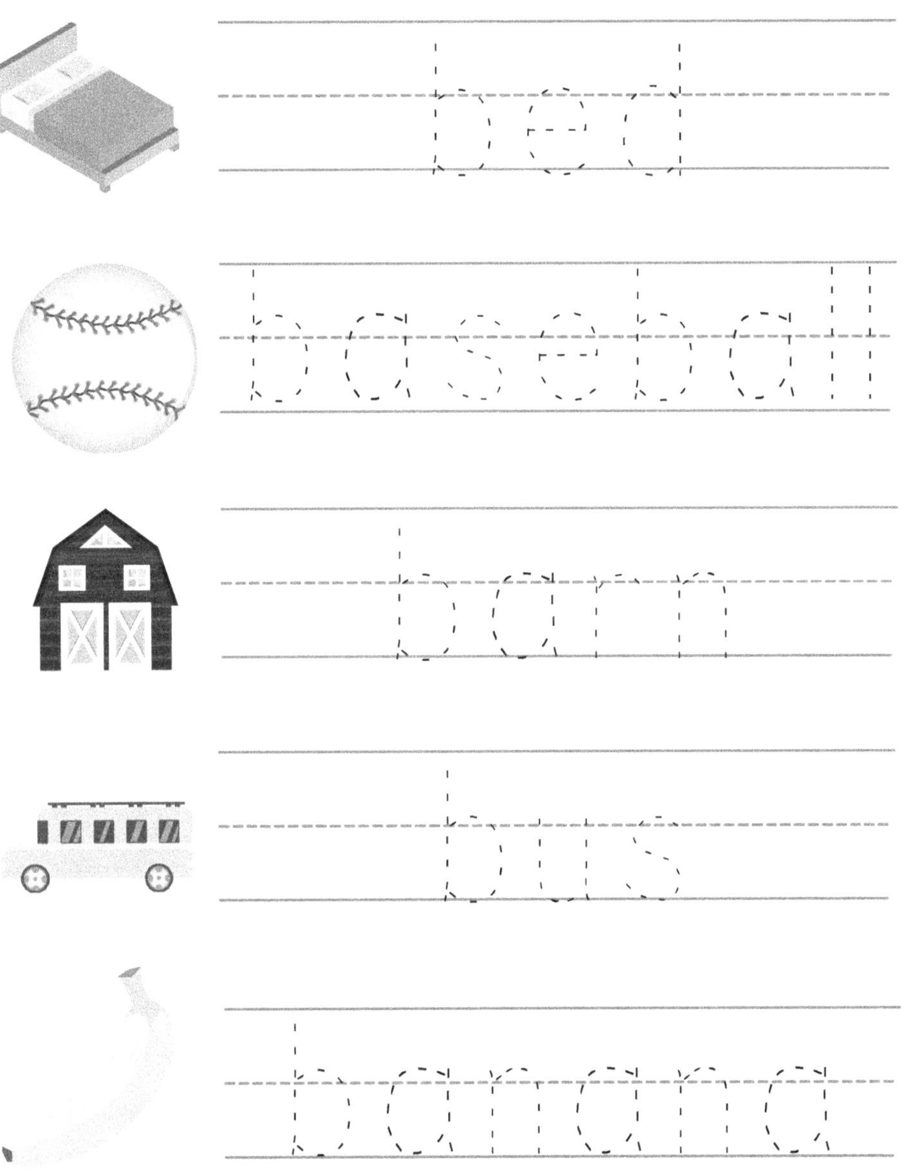

DIRECTIONS: TRACE THE WORDS THAT BEGIN WITH THE LETTER B

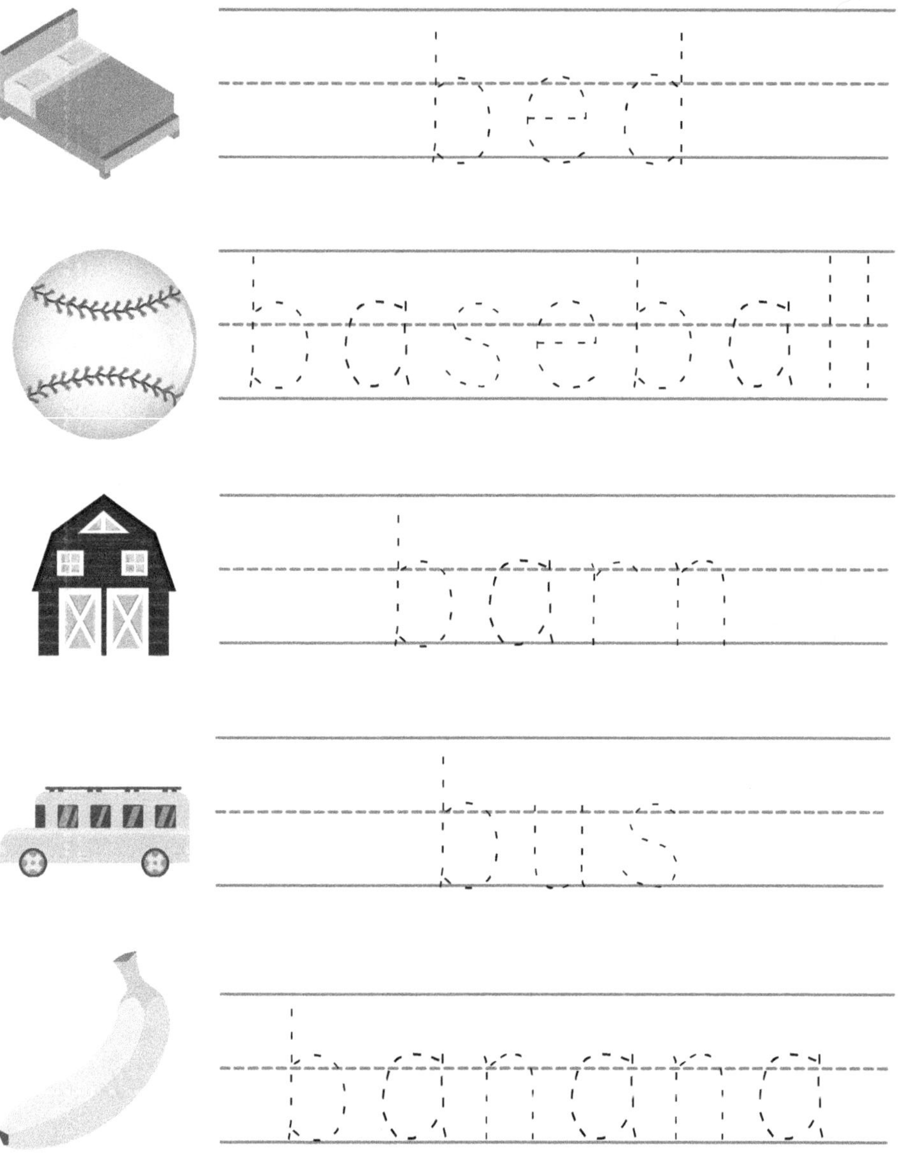

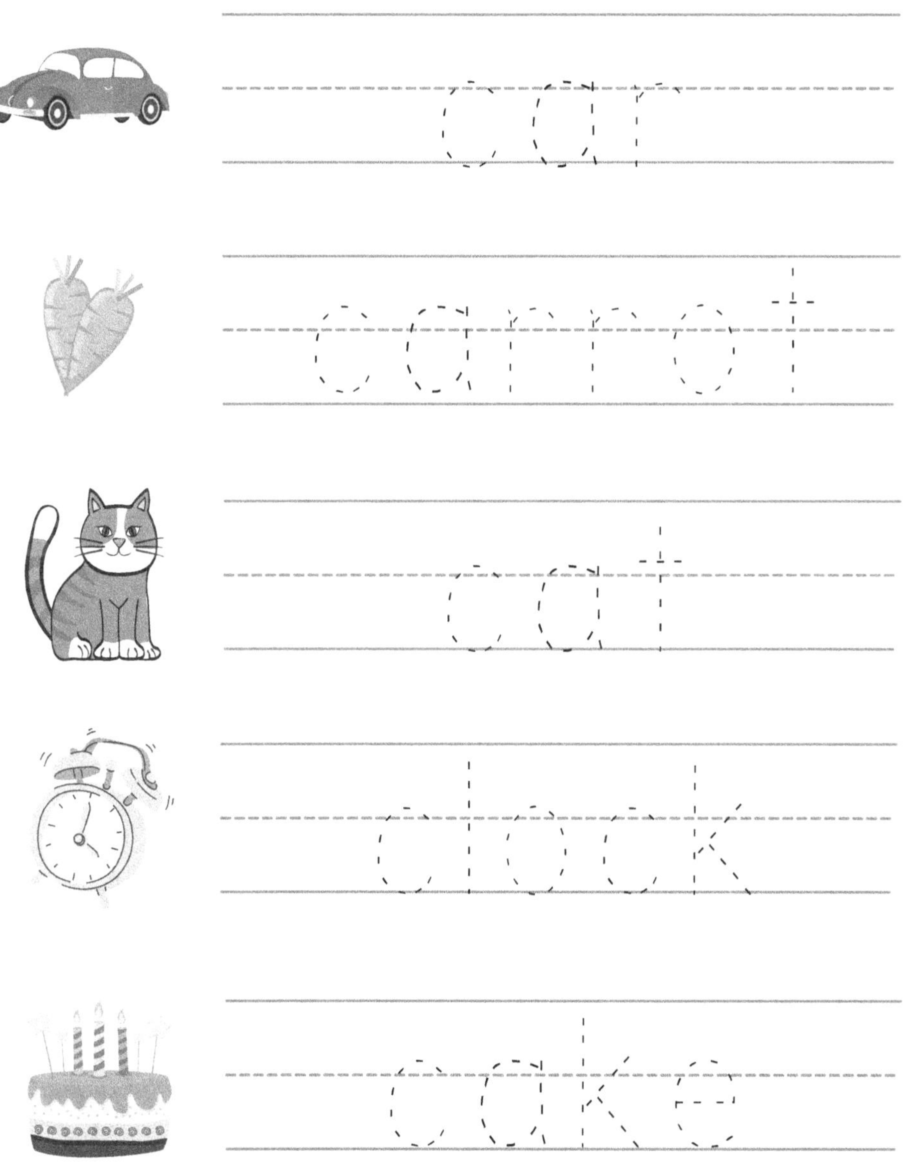

car
carrot
cat
clock
cake

DIRECTIONS: TRACE THE WORDS THAT BEGIN WITH THE LETTER C

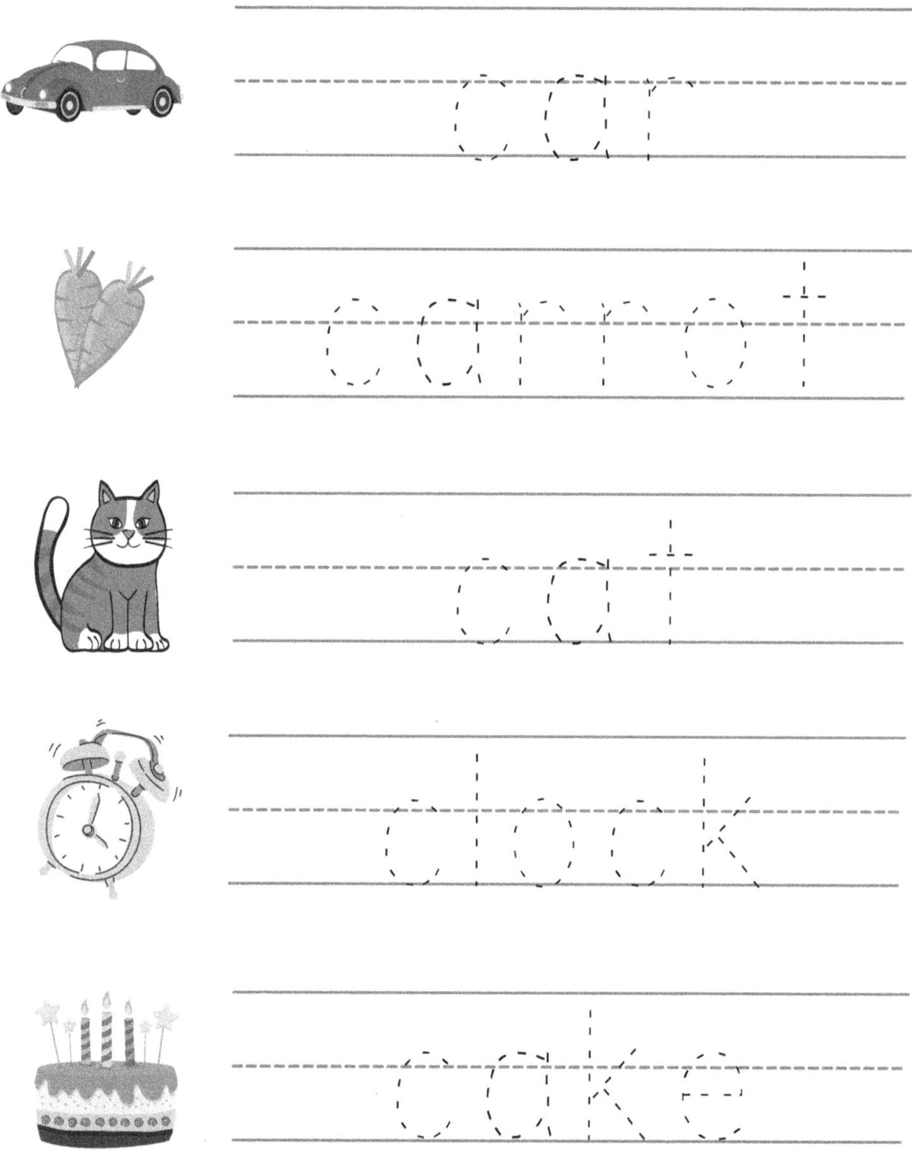

DIRECTIONS: TRACE THE WORDS THAT BEGIN WITH THE LETTER D

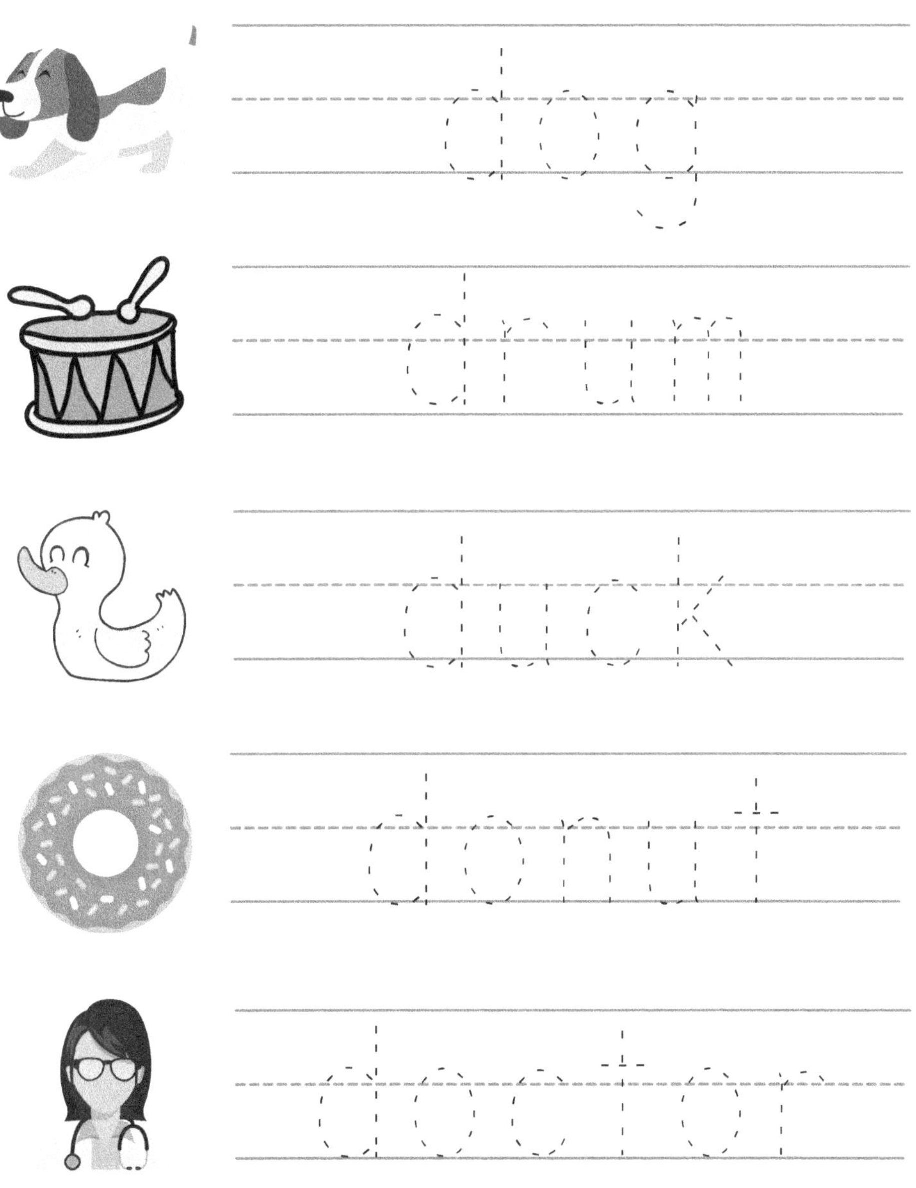

DIRECTIONS: TRACE THE WORDS THAT BEGIN WITH THE LETTER D

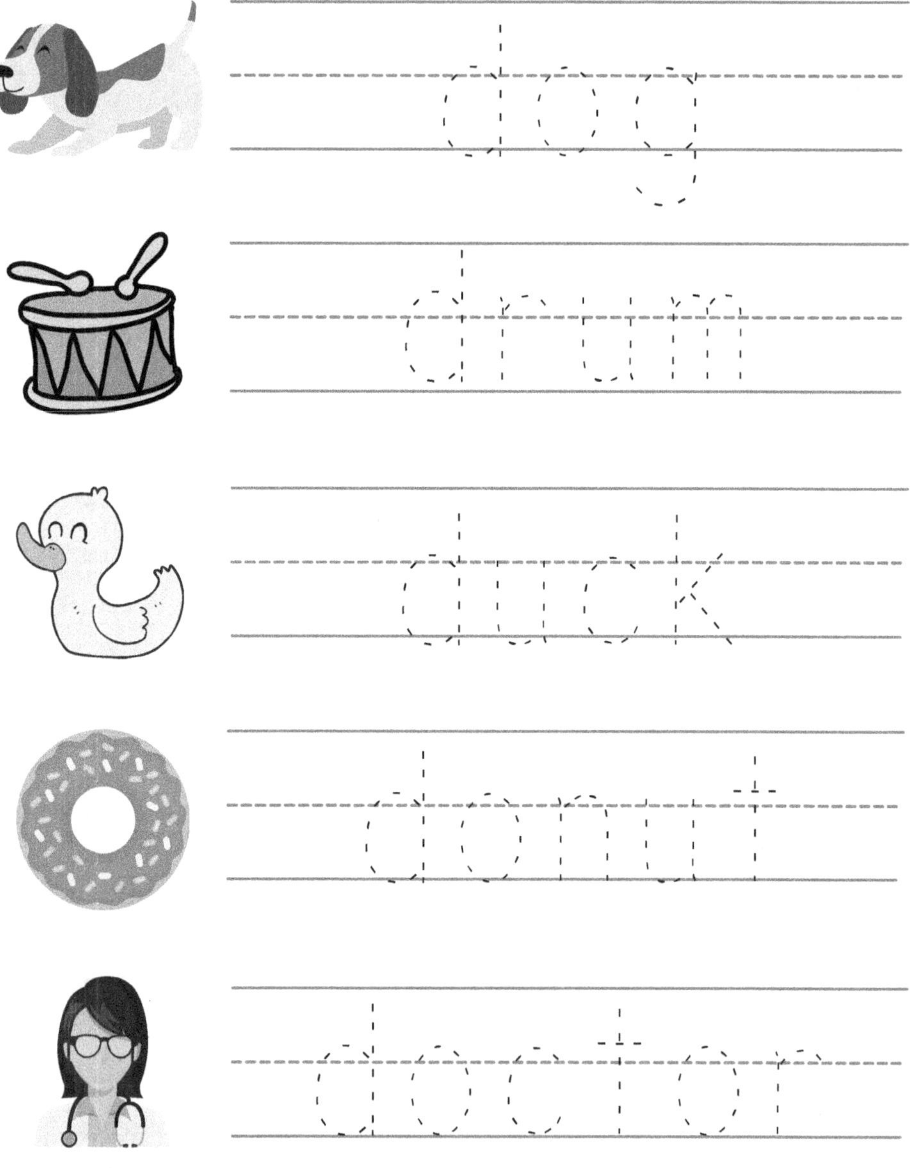

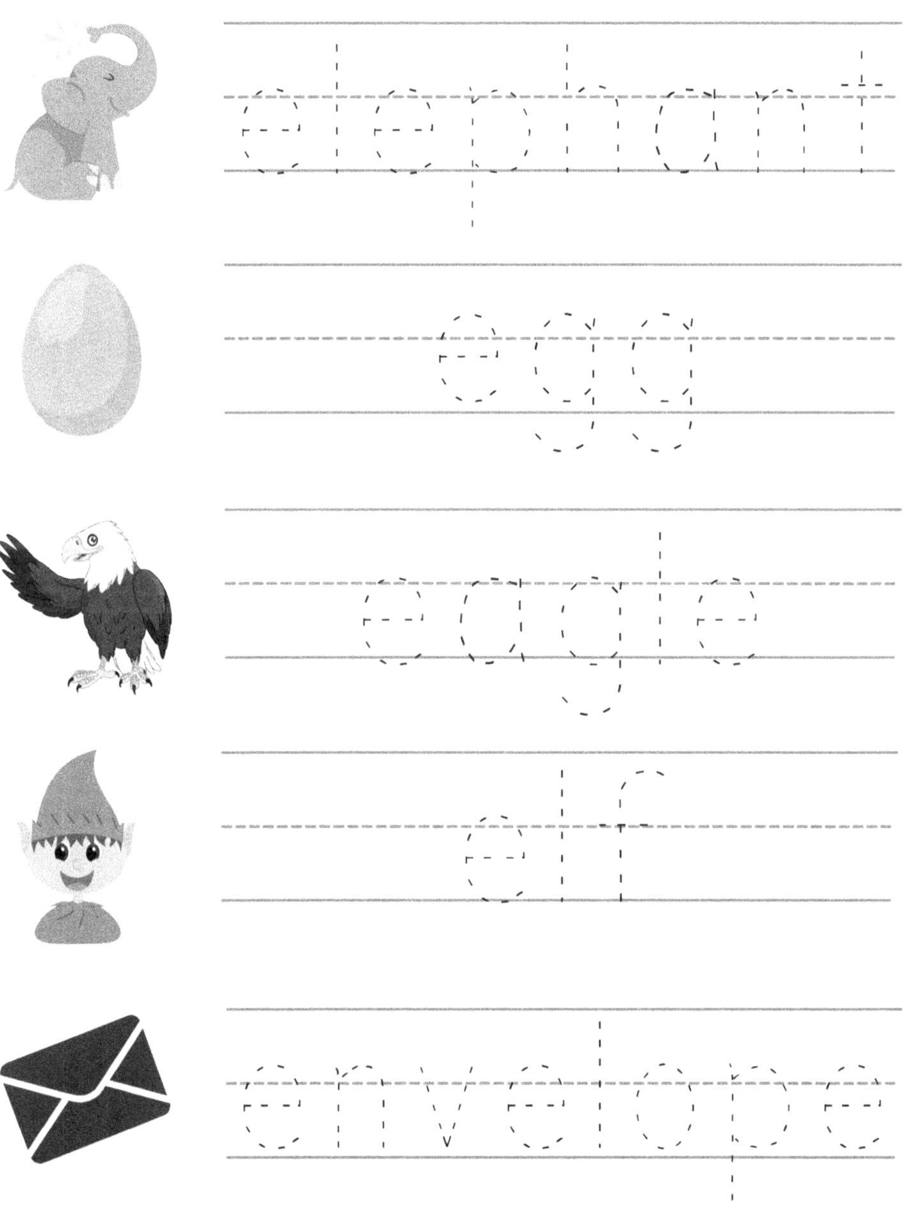

elephant
egg
eagle
elf
envelope

DIRECTIONS: TRACE THE WORDS THAT BEGIN WITH THE LETTER E

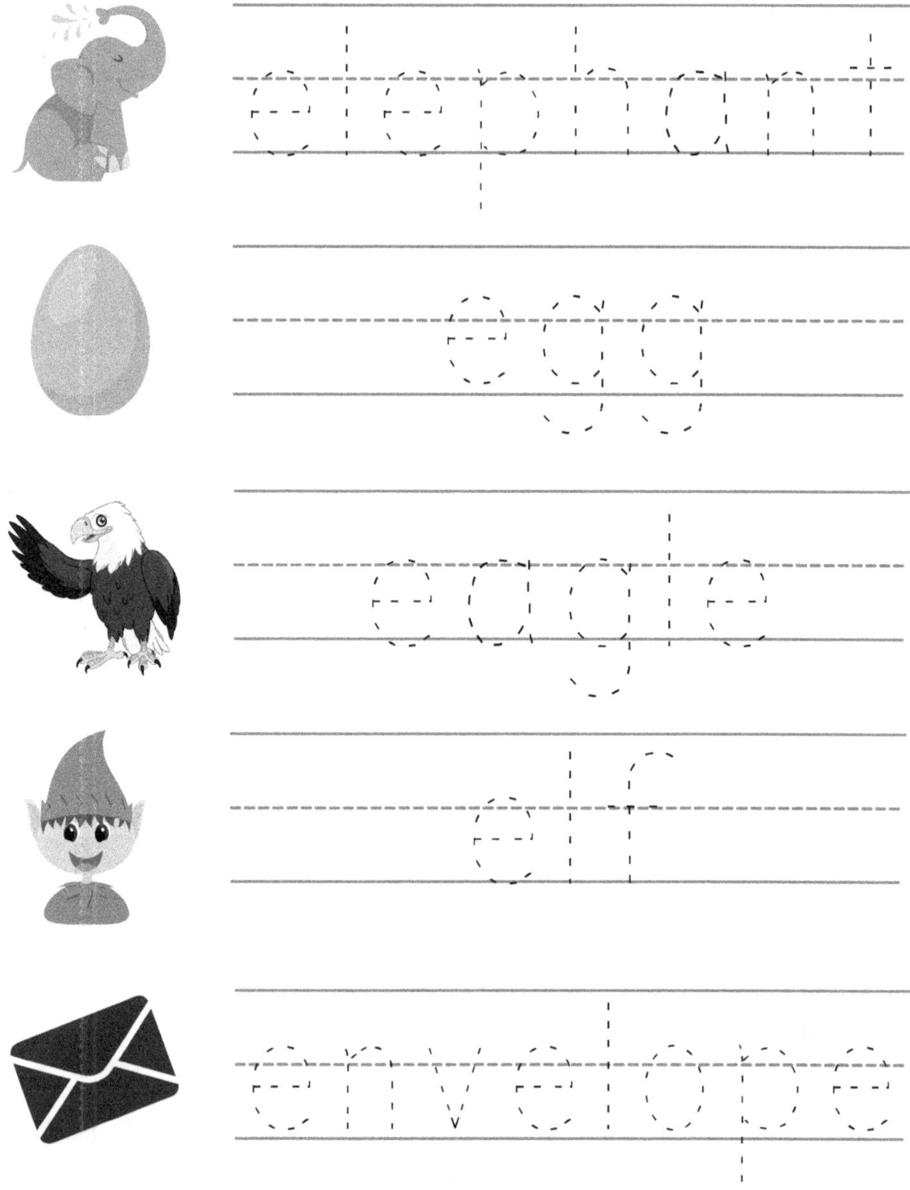

DIRECTIONS: TRACE THE WORDS THAT BEGIN WITH THE LETTER F

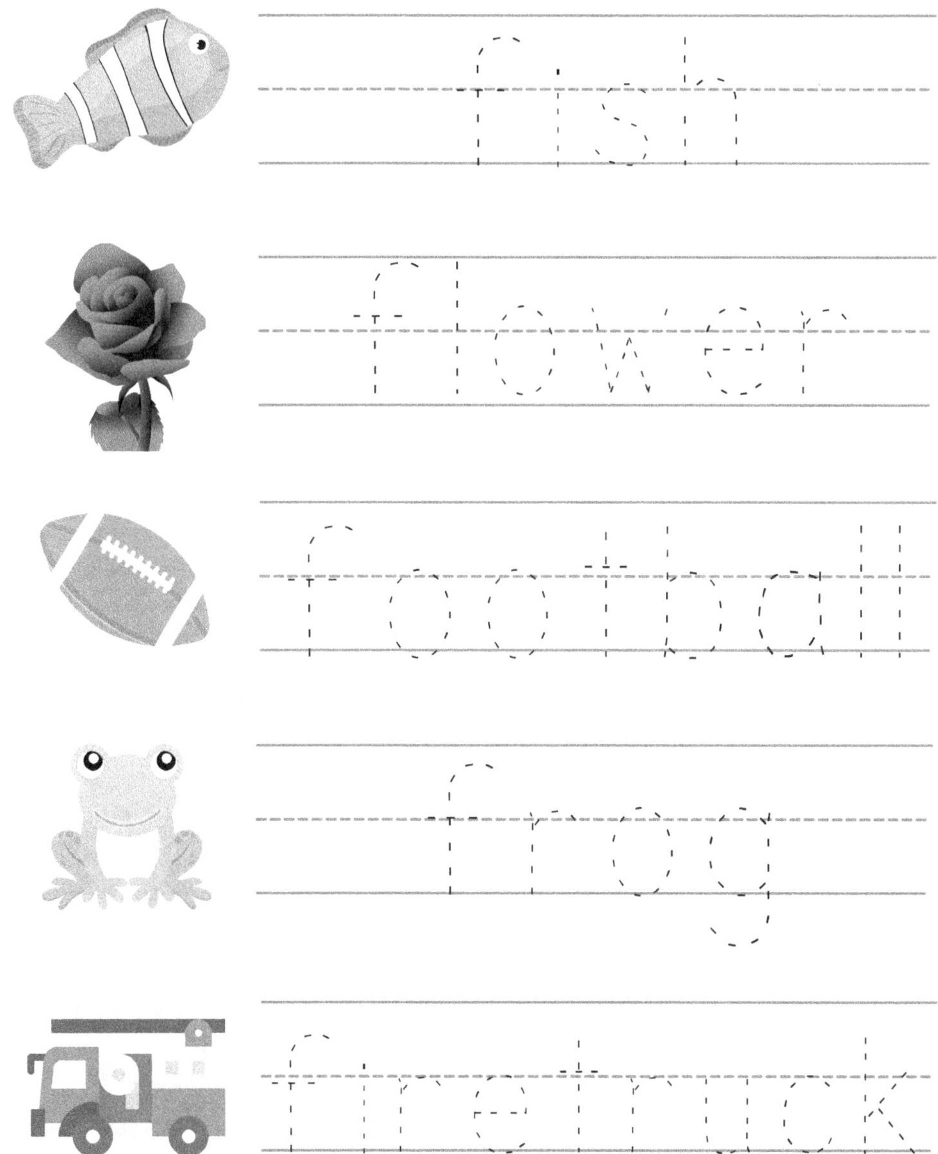

DIRECTIONS: TRACE THE WORDS THAT BEGIN WITH THE LETTER F

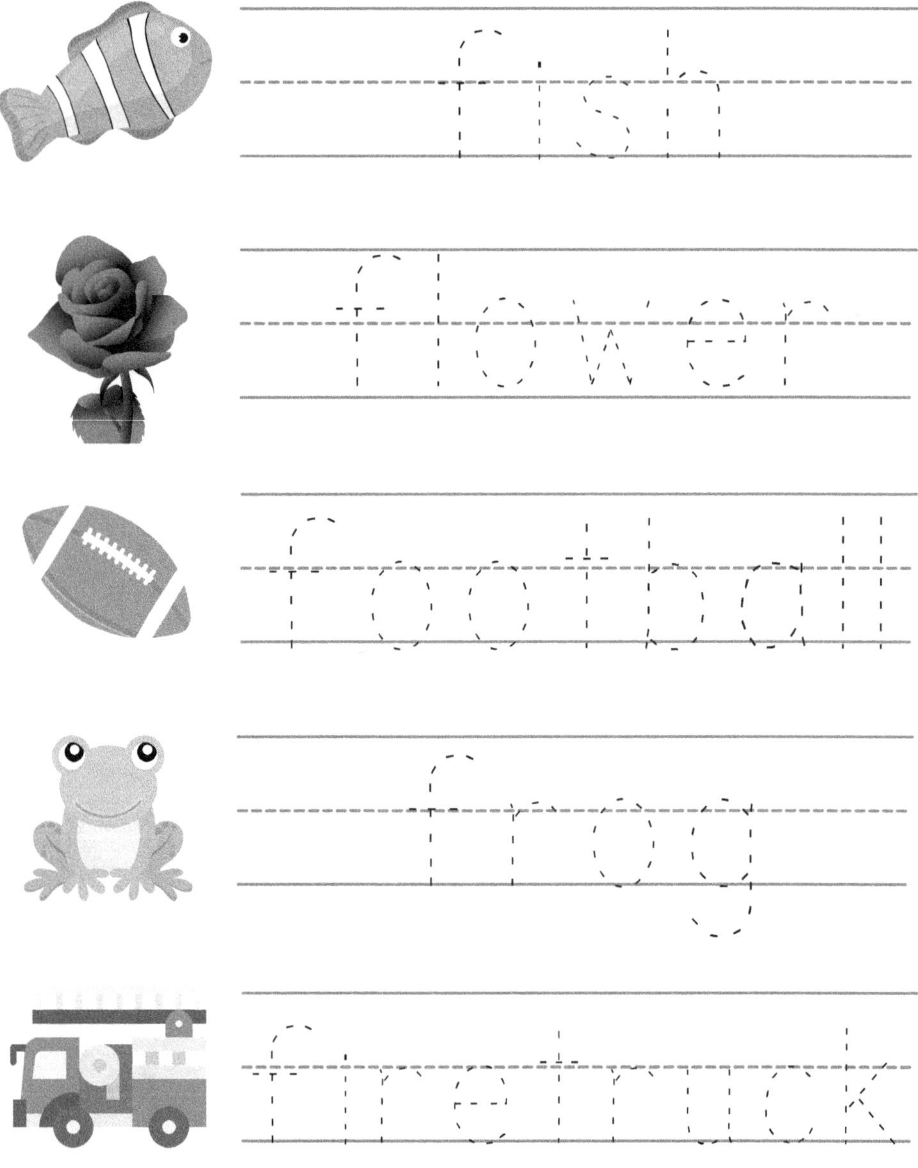

DIRECTIONS: TRACE THE WORDS THAT BEGIN WITH THE LETTER G

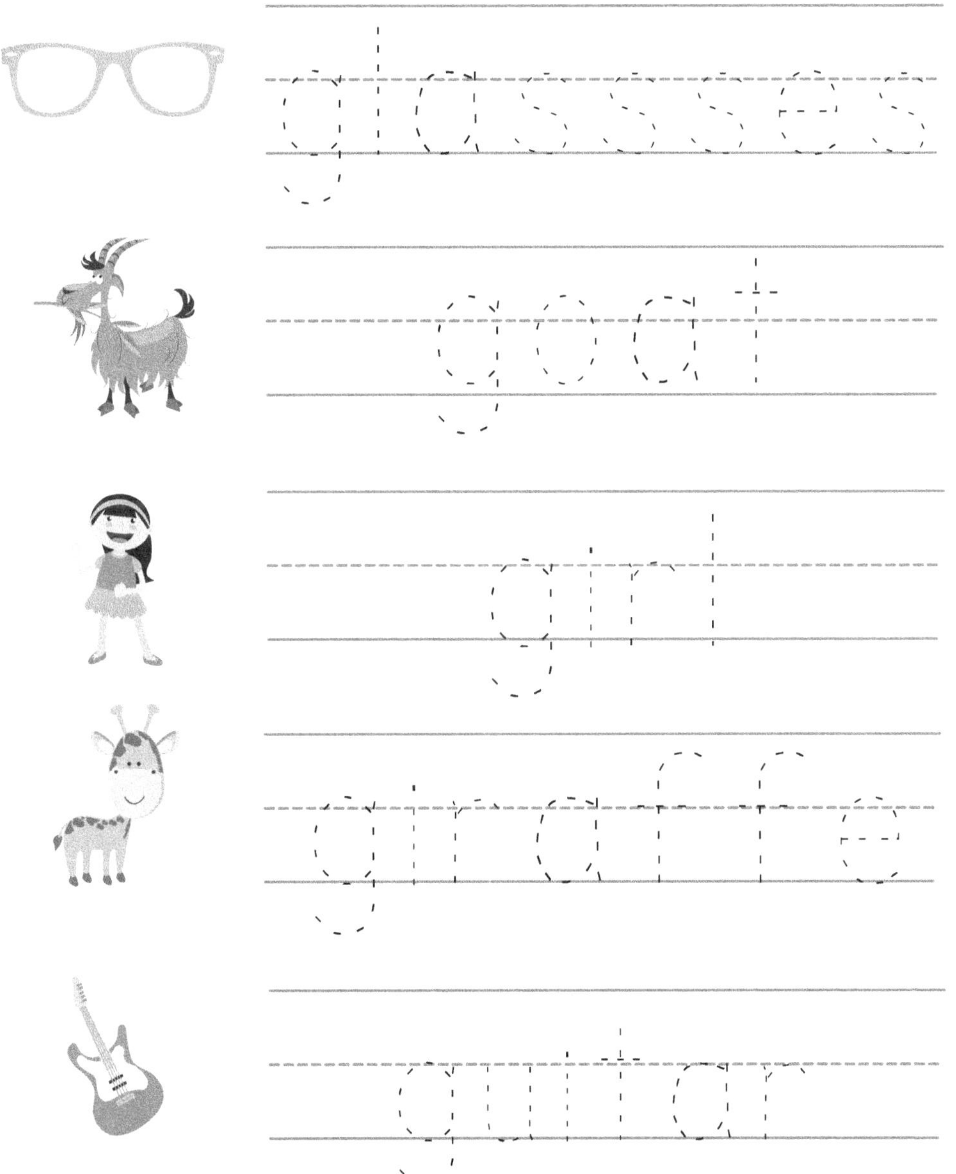

DIRECTIONS: TRACE THE WORDS THAT BEGIN WITH THE LETTER G

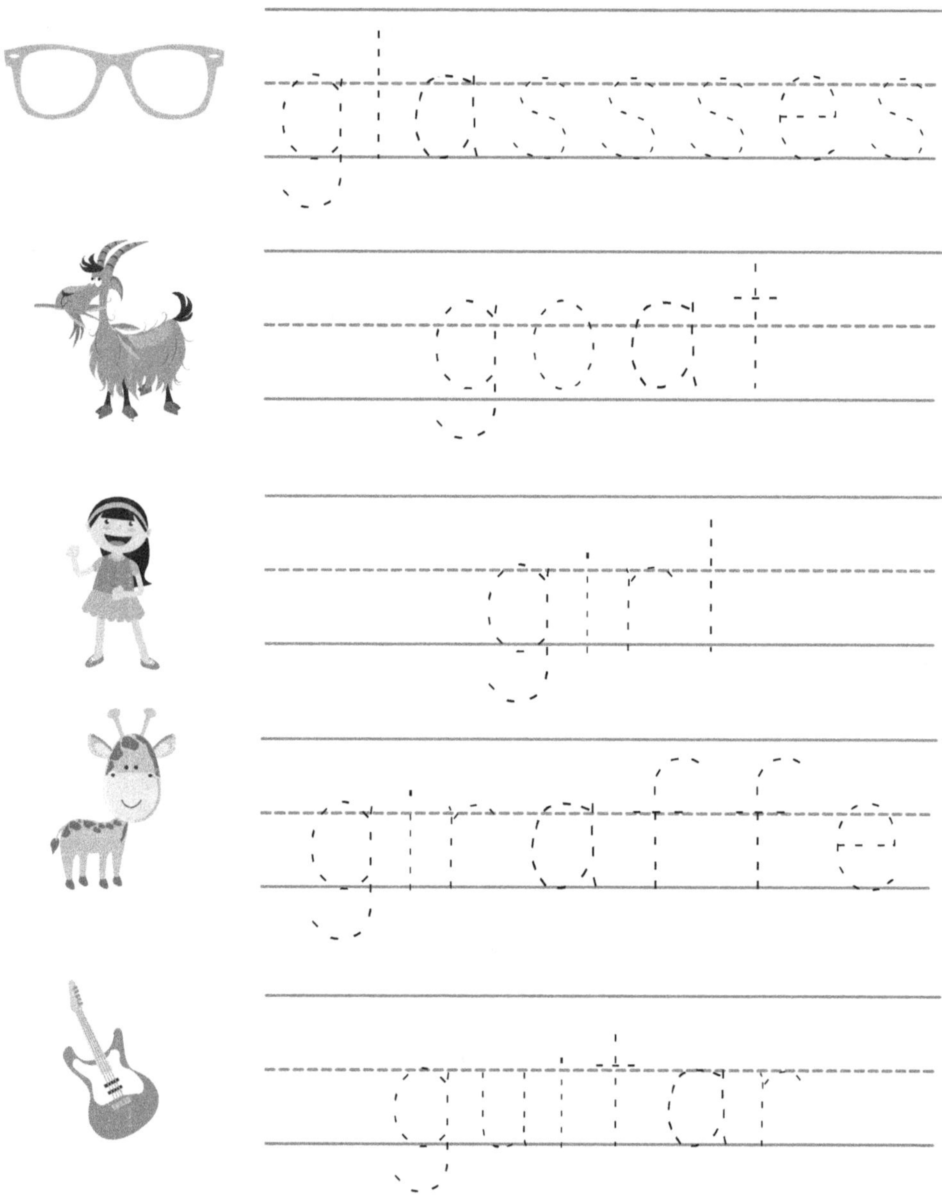

DIRECTIONS: TRACE THE WORDS THAT BEGIN WITH THE LETTER H

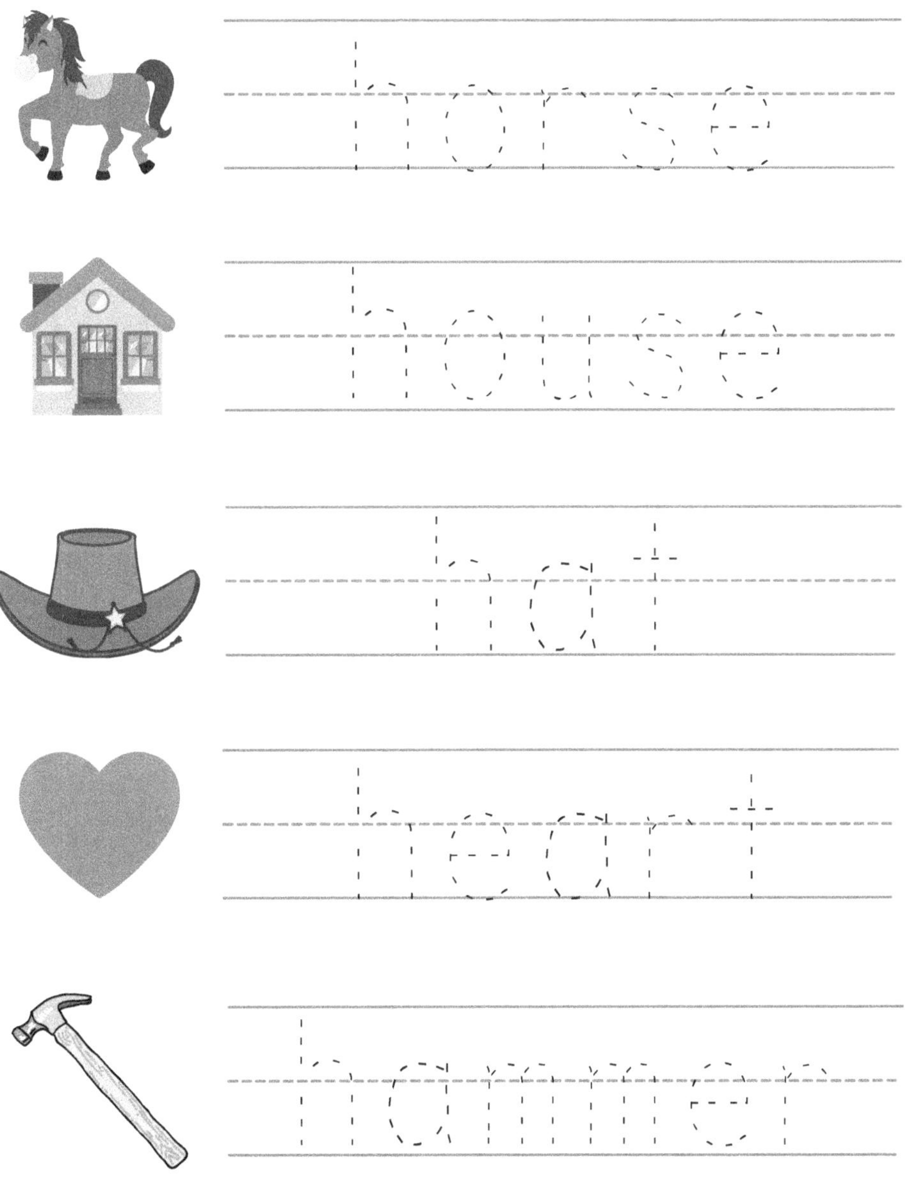

DIRECTIONS: TRACE THE WORDS THAT BEGIN WITH THE LETTER H

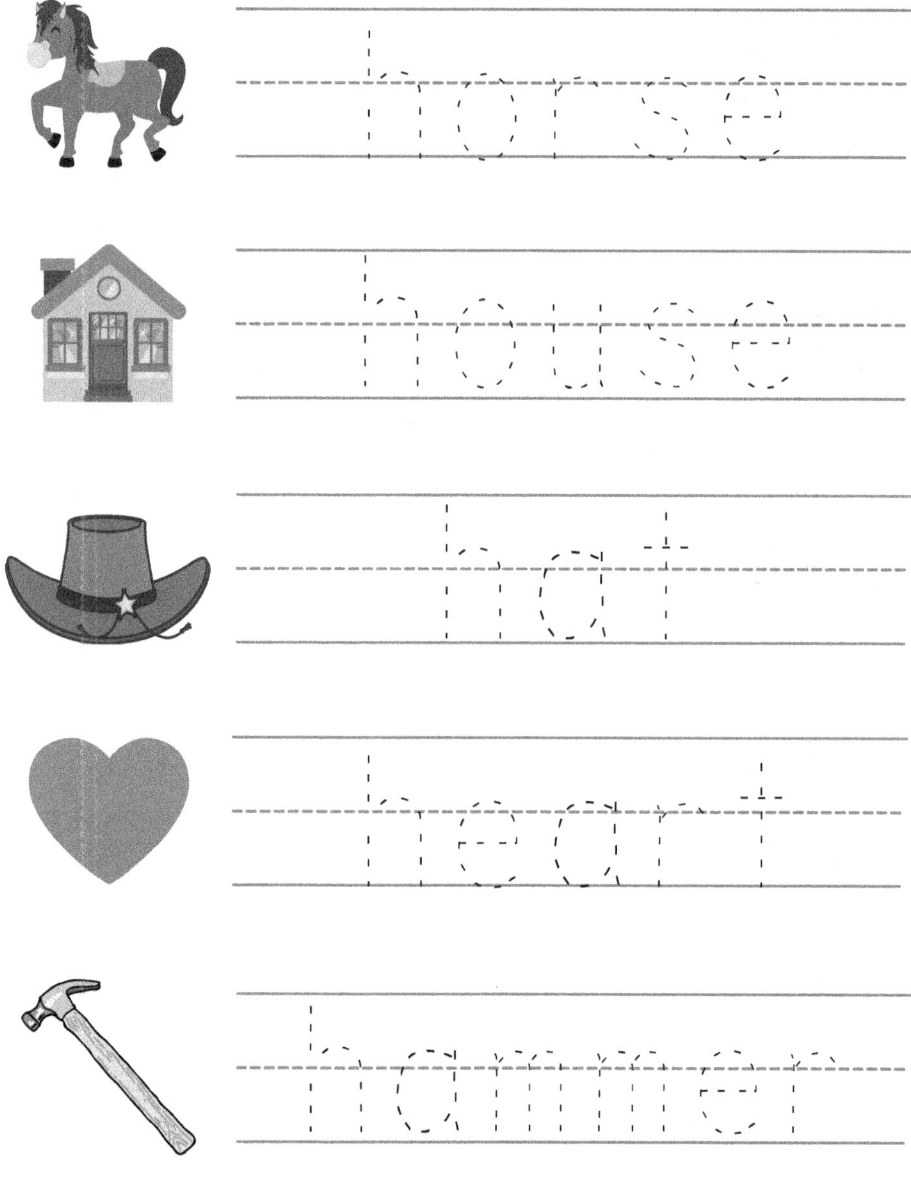

DIRECTIONS: TRACE THE WORDS THAT BEGIN WITH THE LETTER I

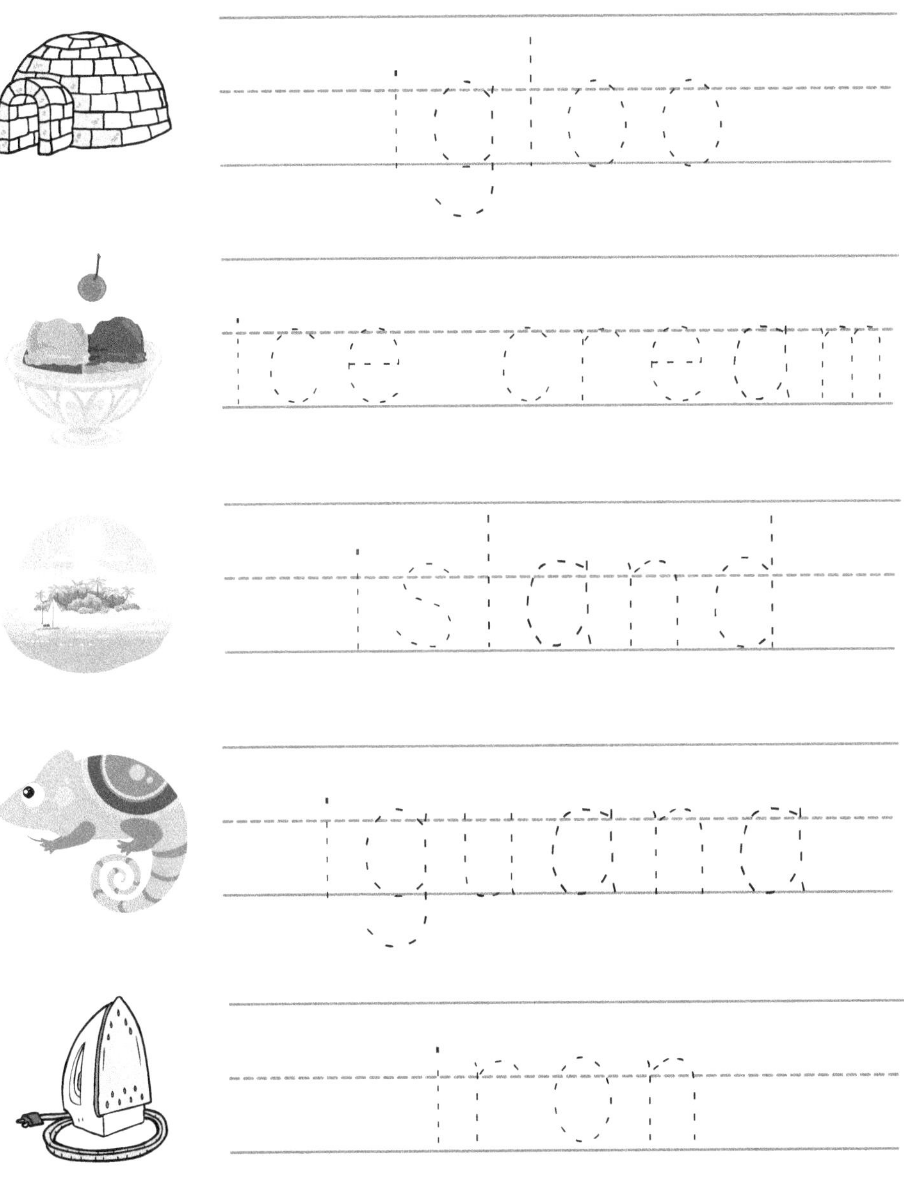

DIRECTIONS: TRACE THE WORDS THAT BEGIN WITH THE
LETTER I

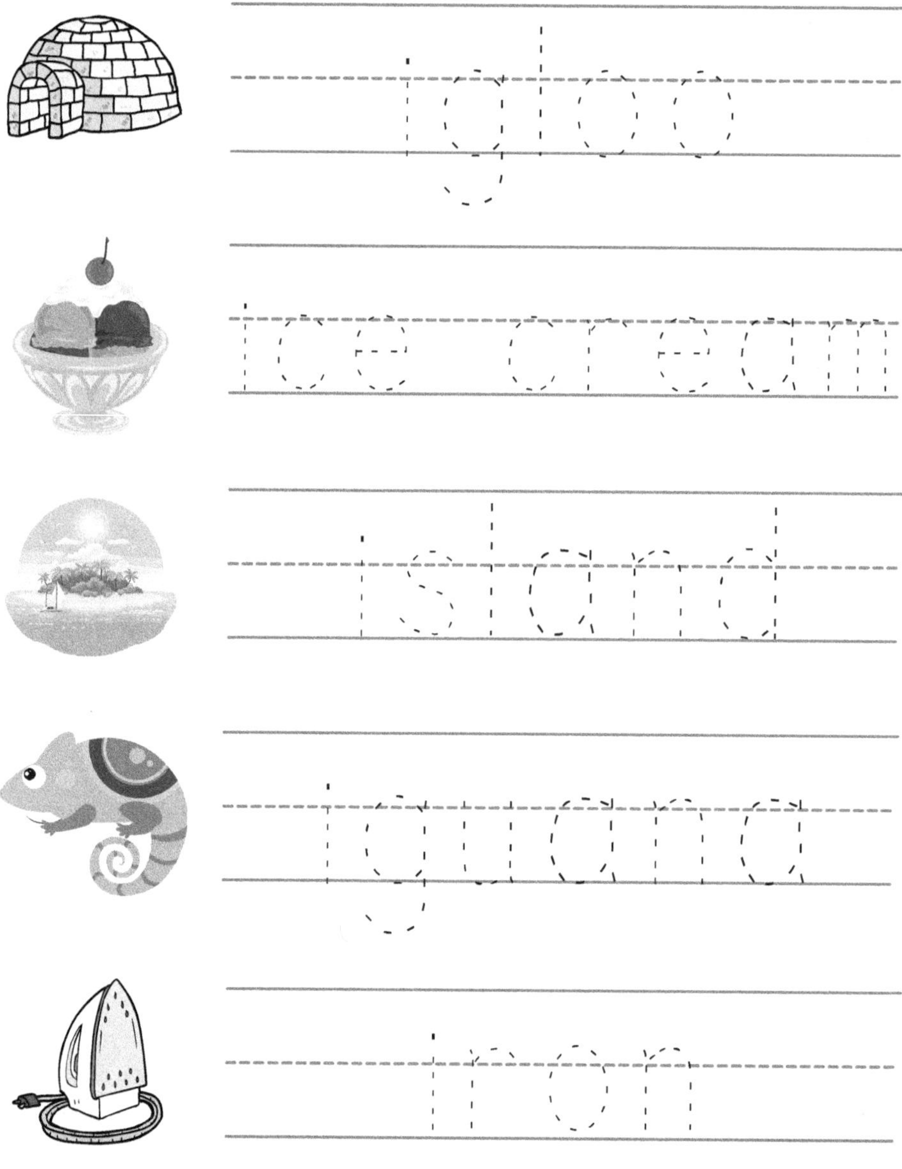
igloo
ice cream
island
iguana
iron

DIRECTIONS: TRACE THE WORDS THAT BEGIN WITH THE LETTER J

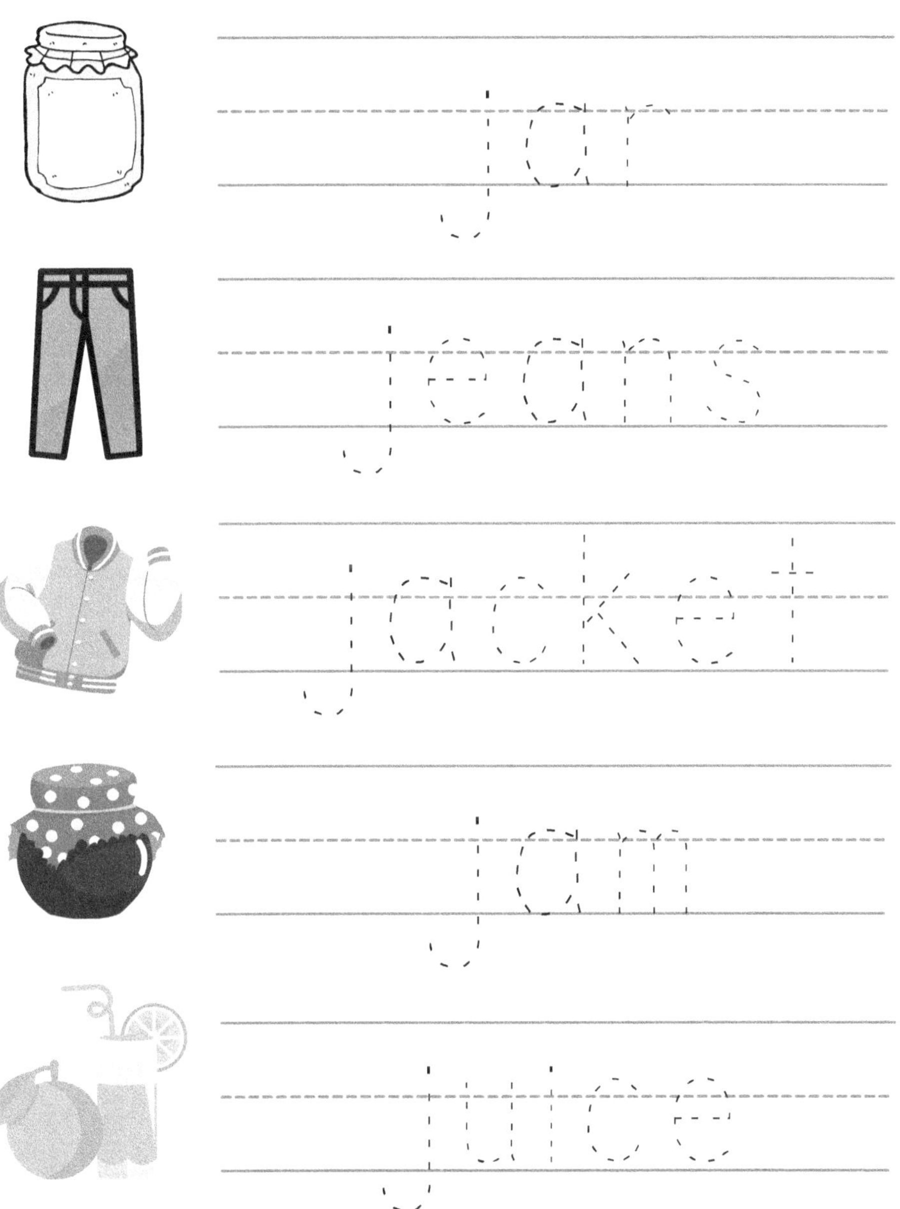

DIRECTIONS: TRACE THE WORDS THAT BEGIN WITH THE LETTER J

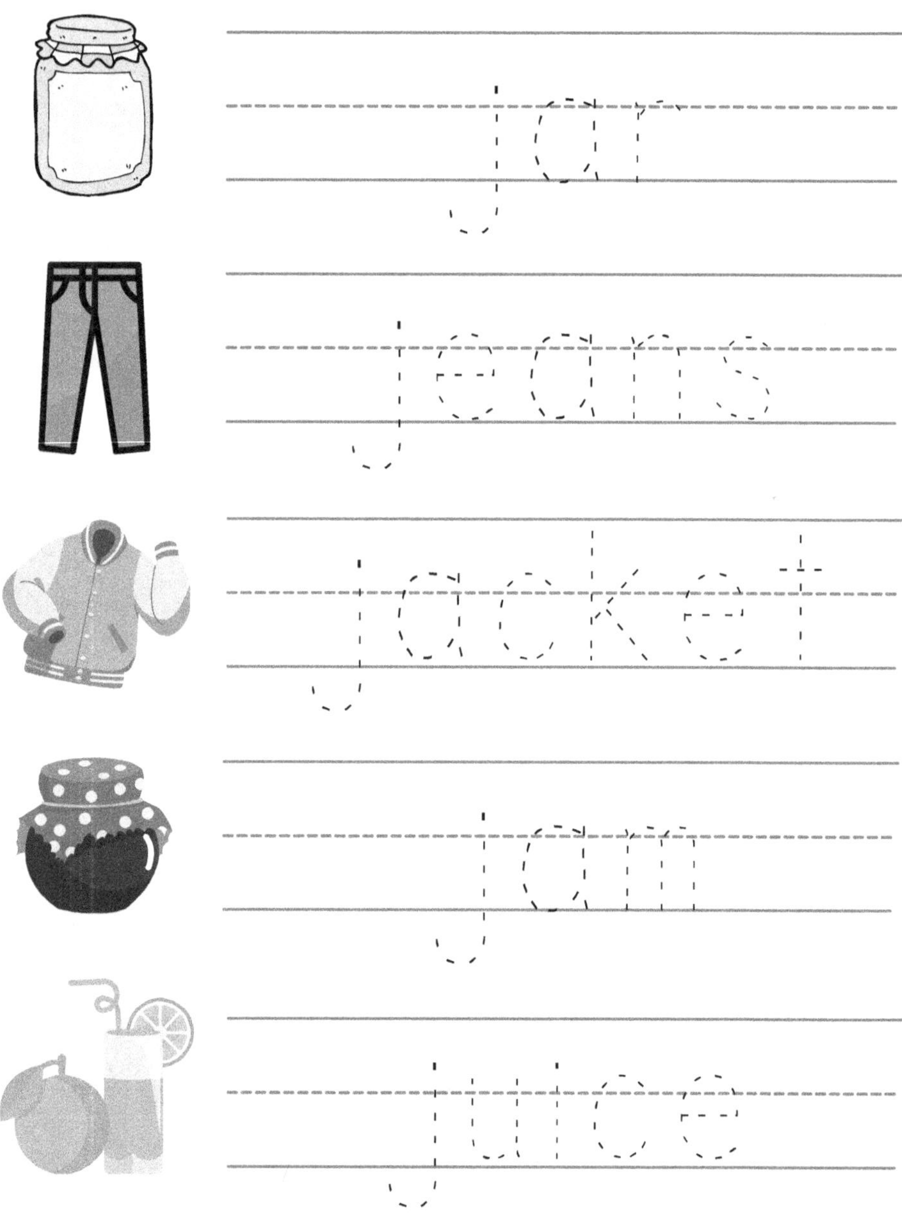

DIRECTIONS: TRACE THE WORDS THAT BEGIN WITH THE LETTER K

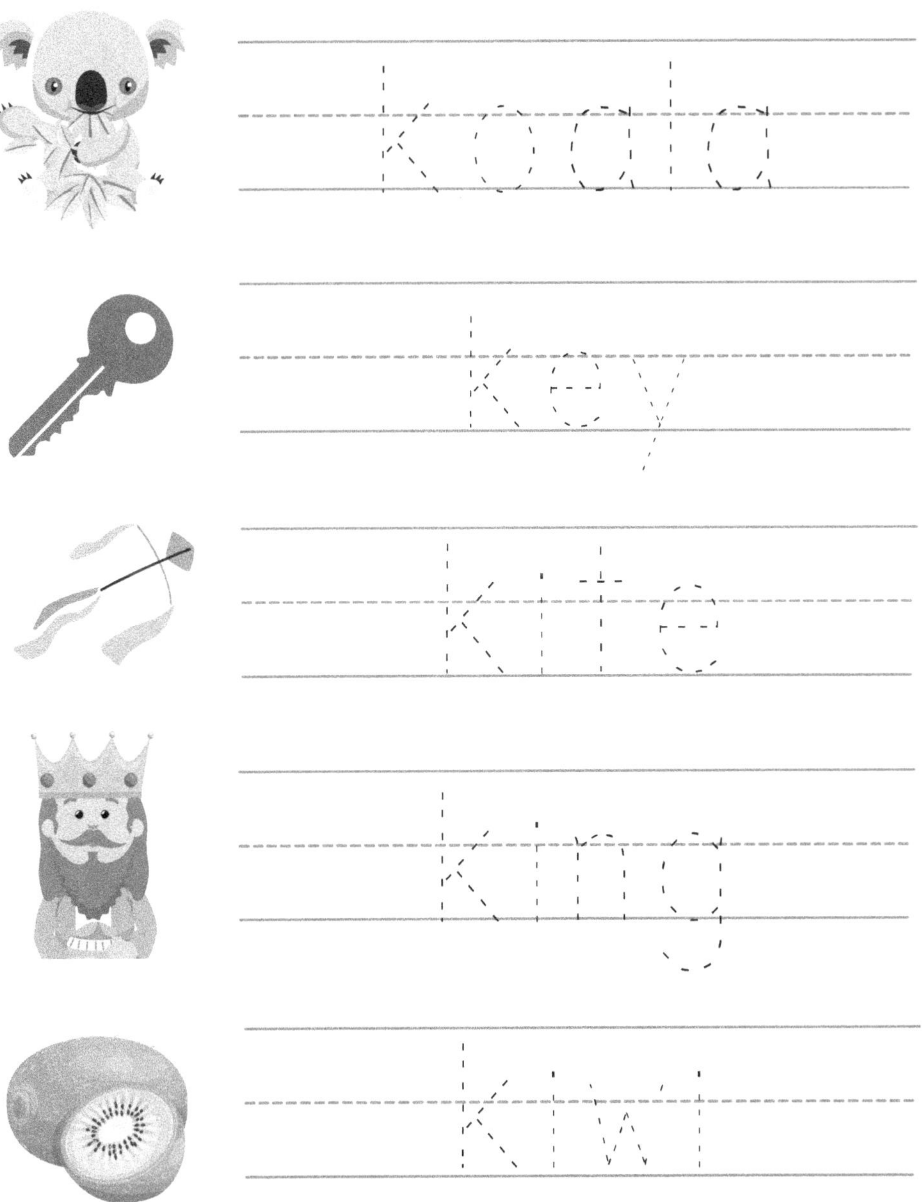

DIRECTIONS: TRACE THE WORDS THAT BEGIN WITH THE LETTER K

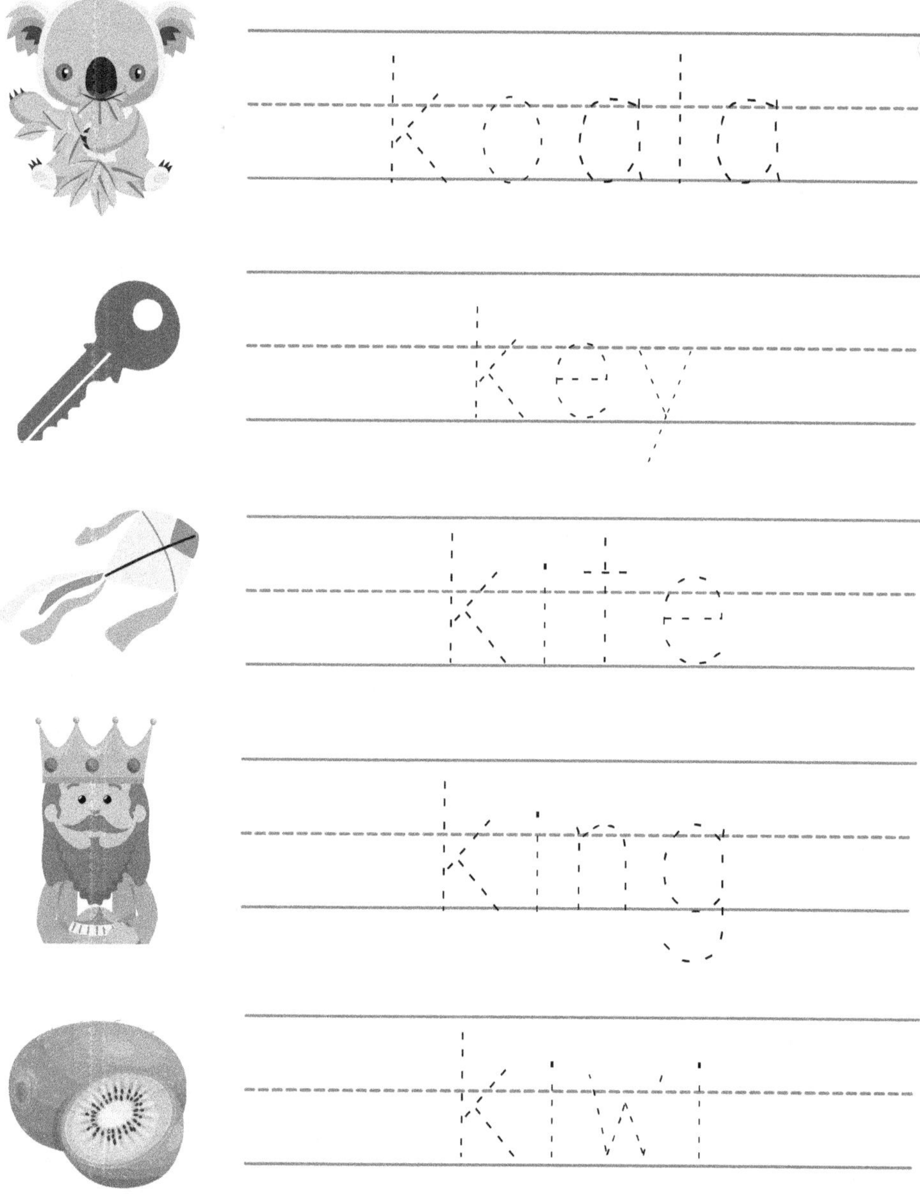

DIRECTIONS: TRACE THE WORDS THAT BEGIN WITH THE LETTER L

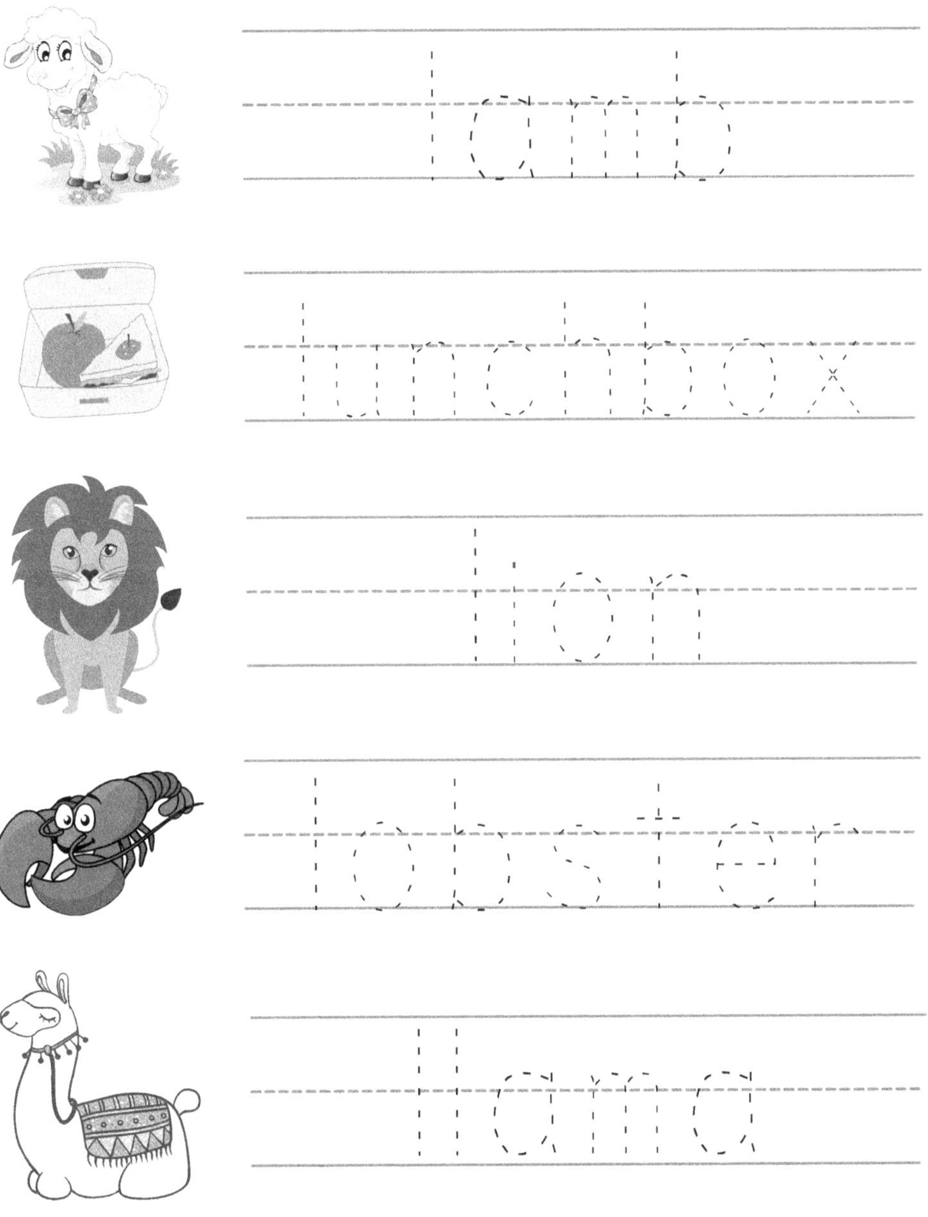

DIRECTIONS: TRACE THE WORDS THAT BEGIN WITH THE LETTER L

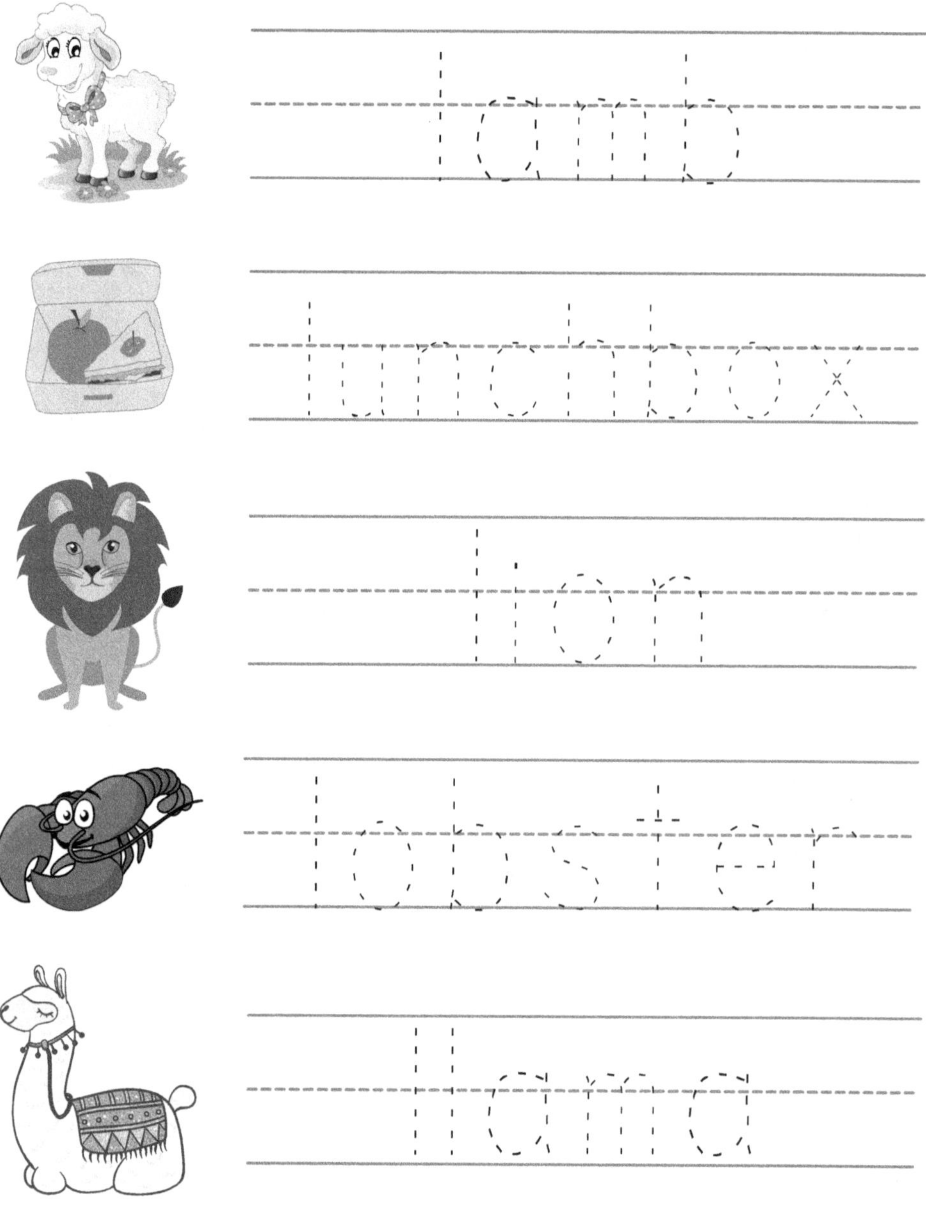

DIRECTIONS: TRACE THE WORDS THAT BEGIN WITH THE LETTER M

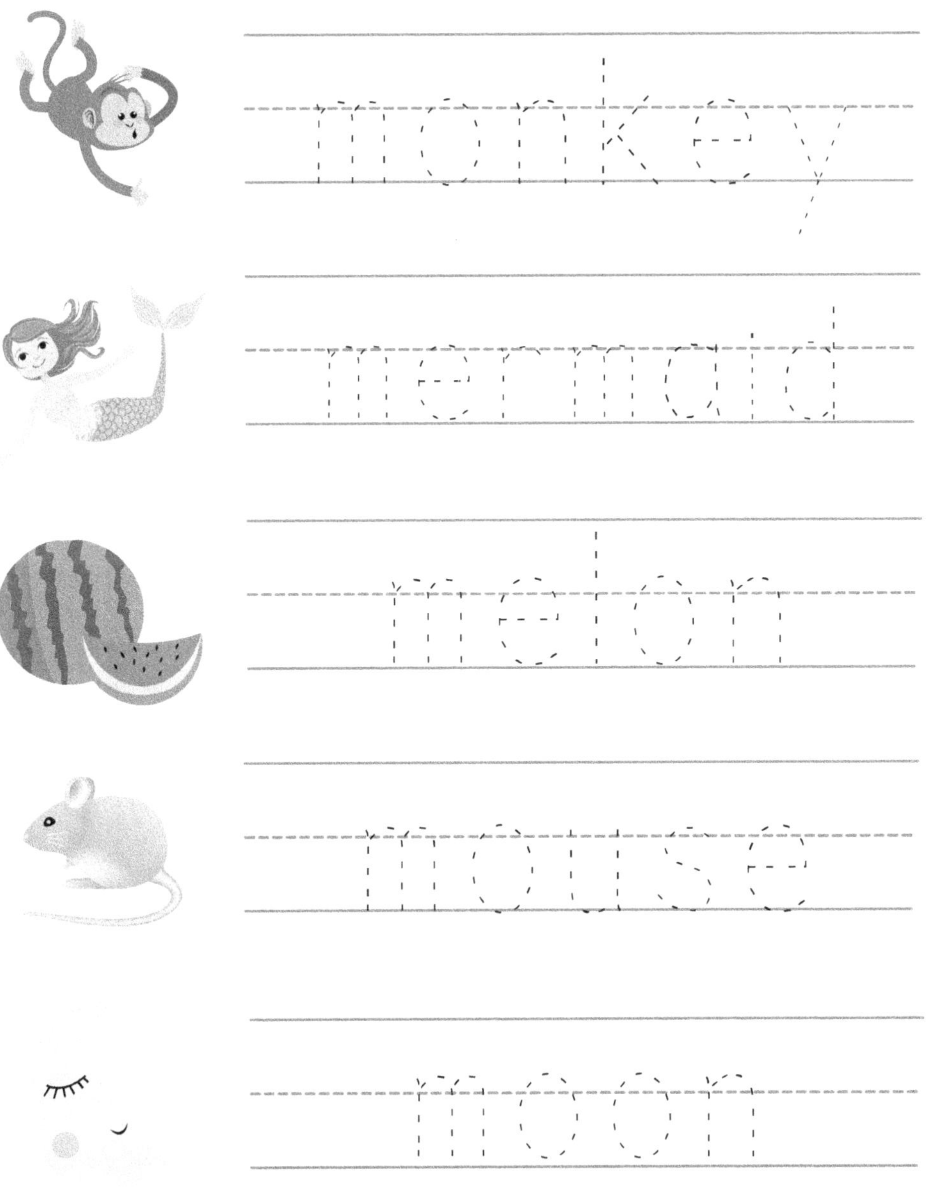

DIRECTIONS: TRACE THE WORDS THAT BEGIN WITH THE LETTER M

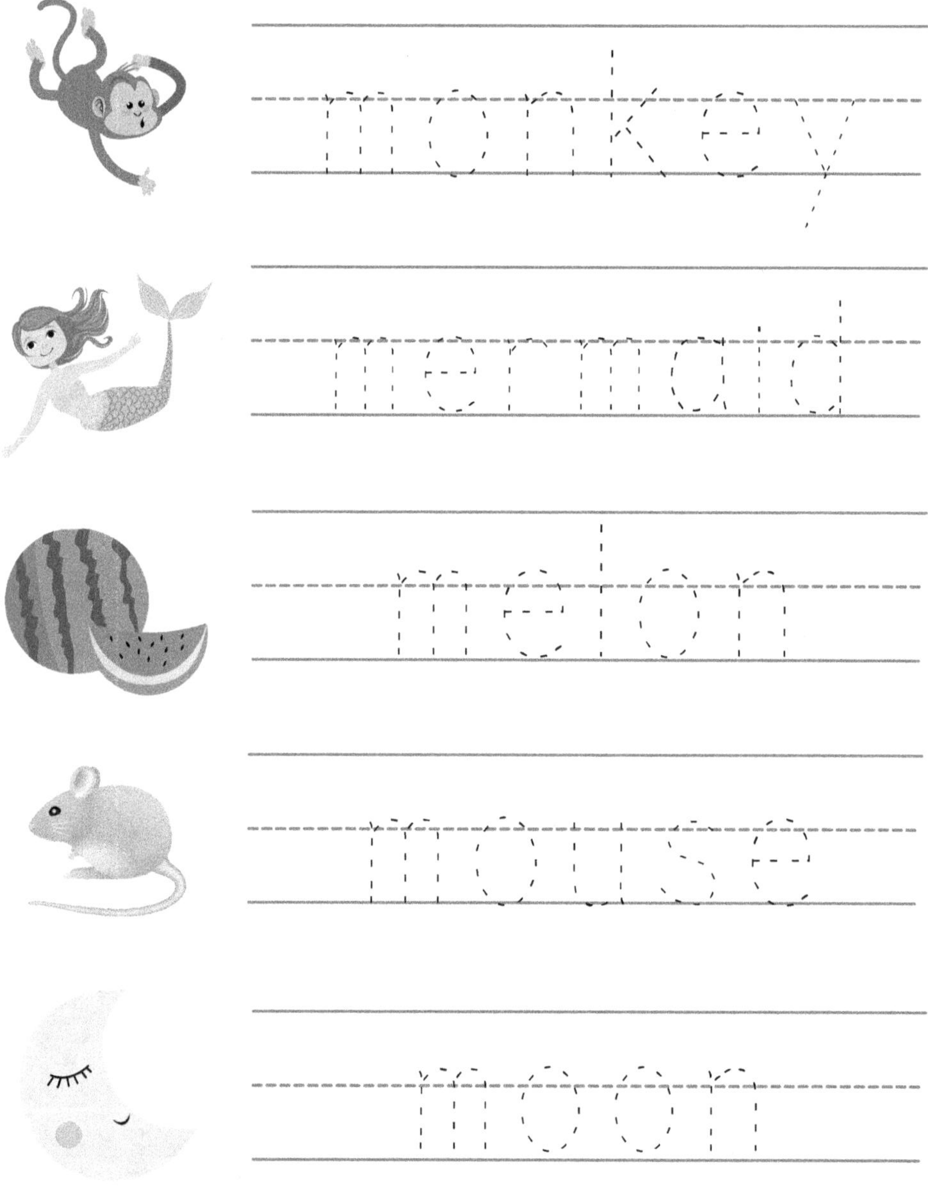

DIRECTIONS: TRACE THE WORDS THAT BEGIN WITH THE LETTER N

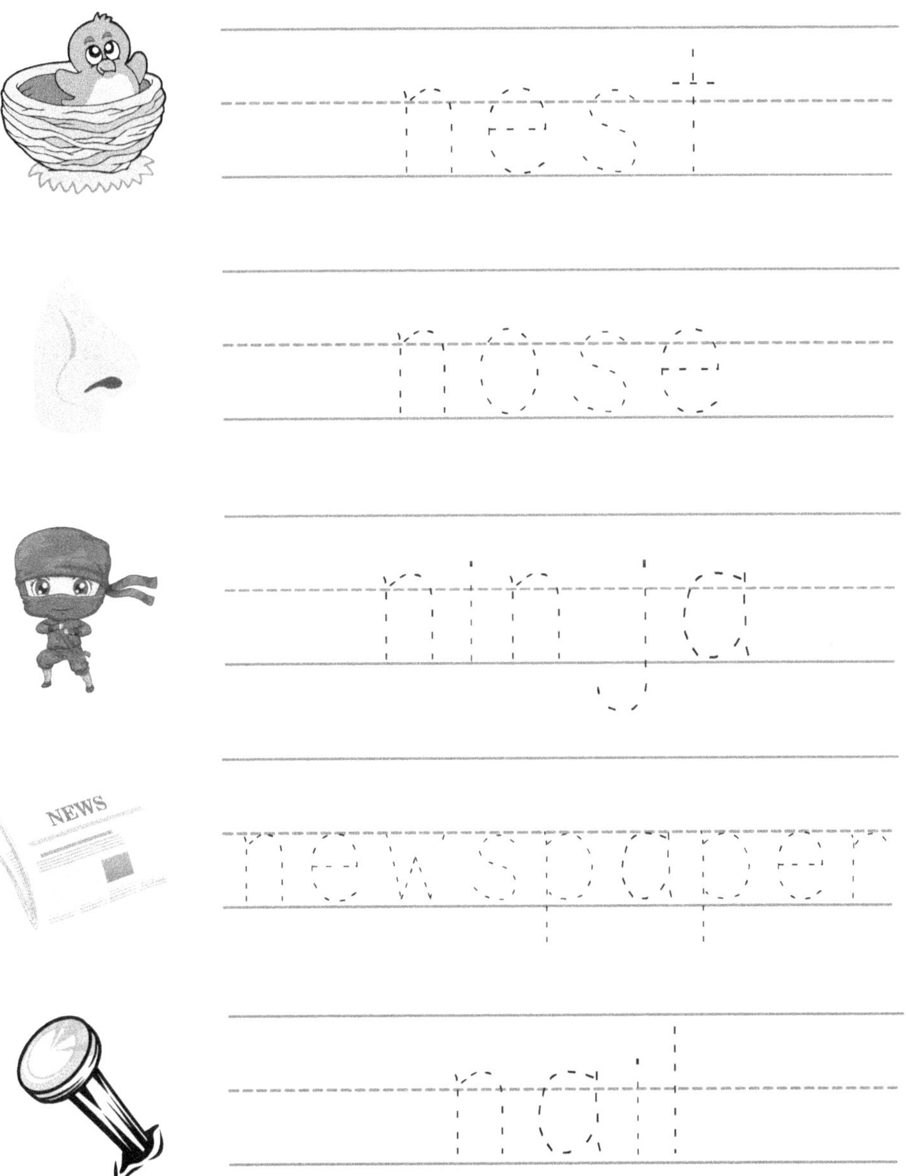

DIRECTIONS: TRACE THE WORDS THAT BEGIN WITH THE LETTER N

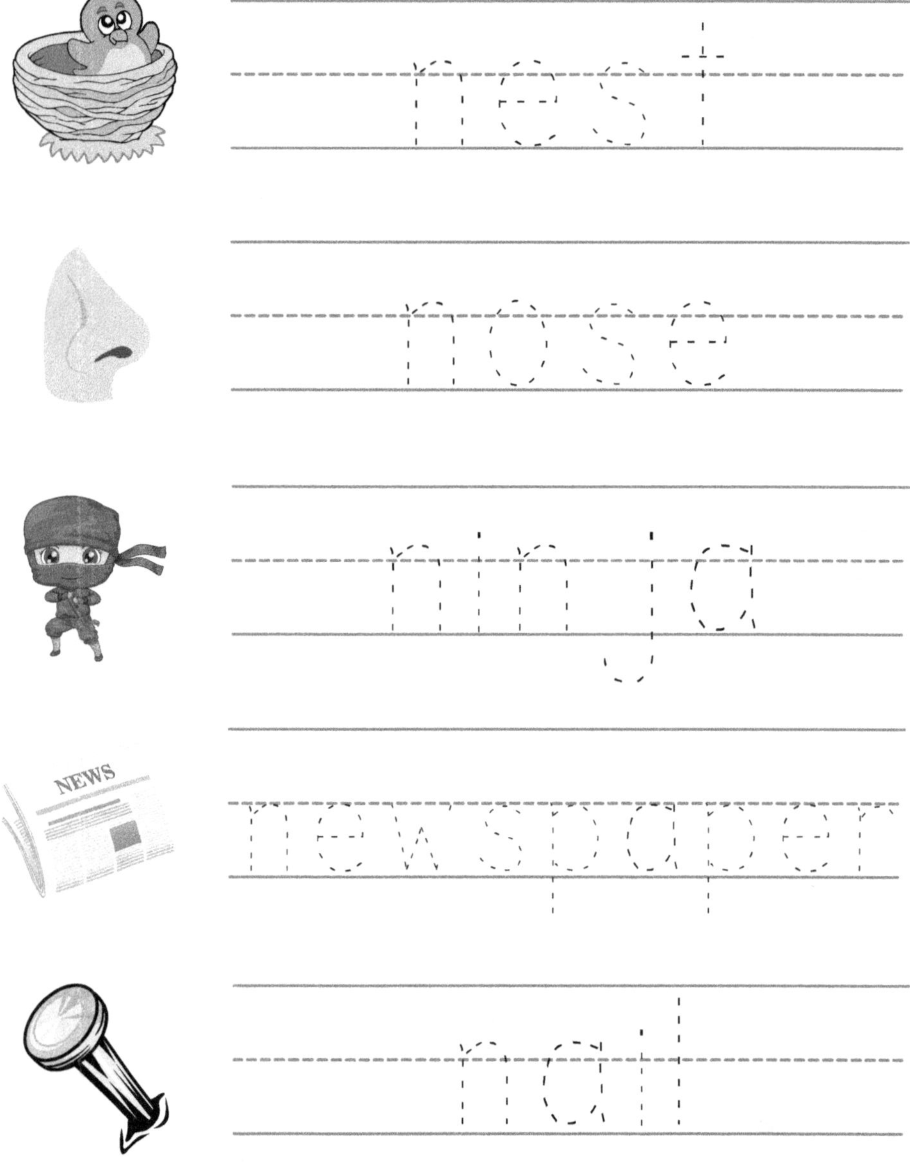

DIRECTIONS: TRACE THE WORDS THAT BEGIN WITH THE
LETTER O

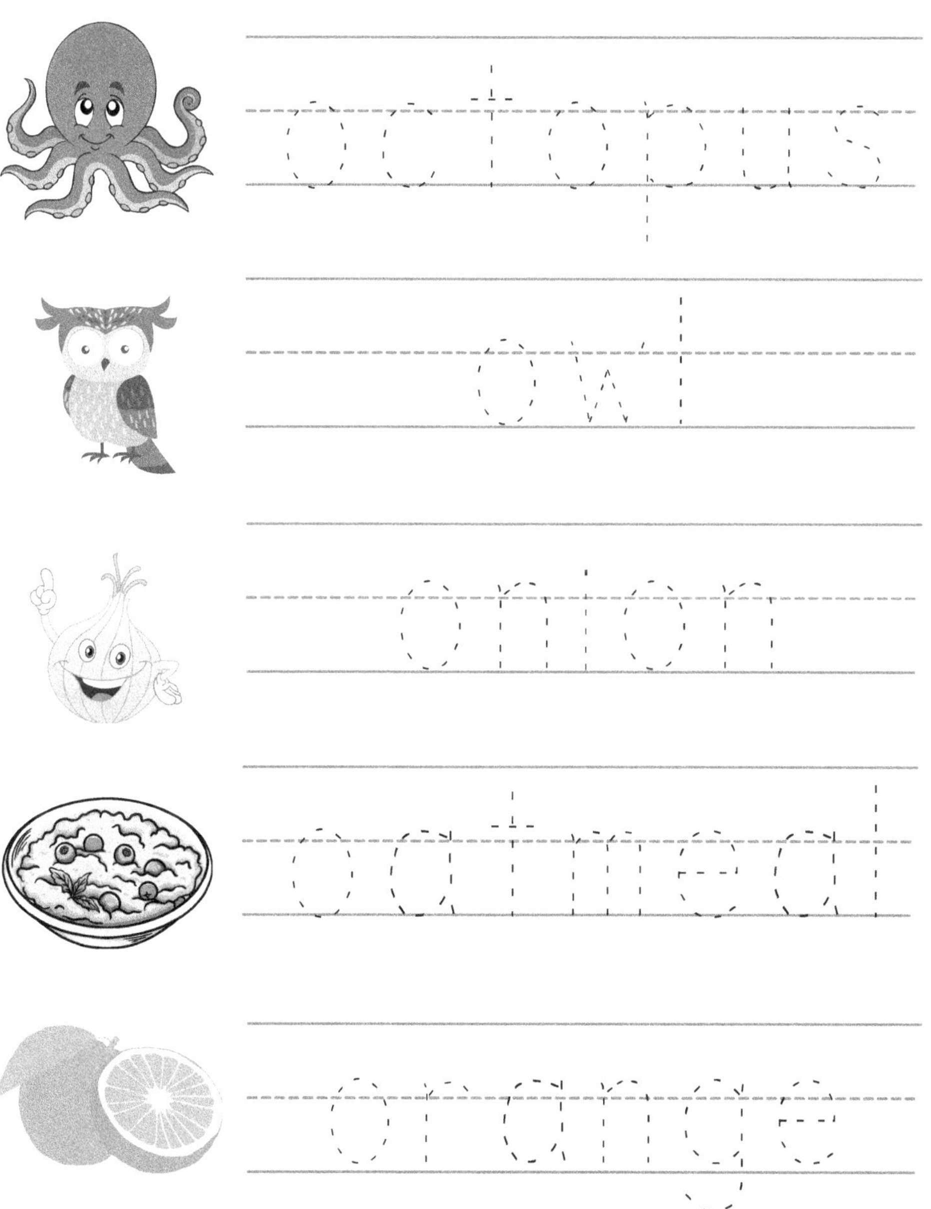

octopus
owl
onion
oatmeal
orange

DIRECTIONS: TRACE THE WORDS THAT BEGIN WITH THE LETTER O

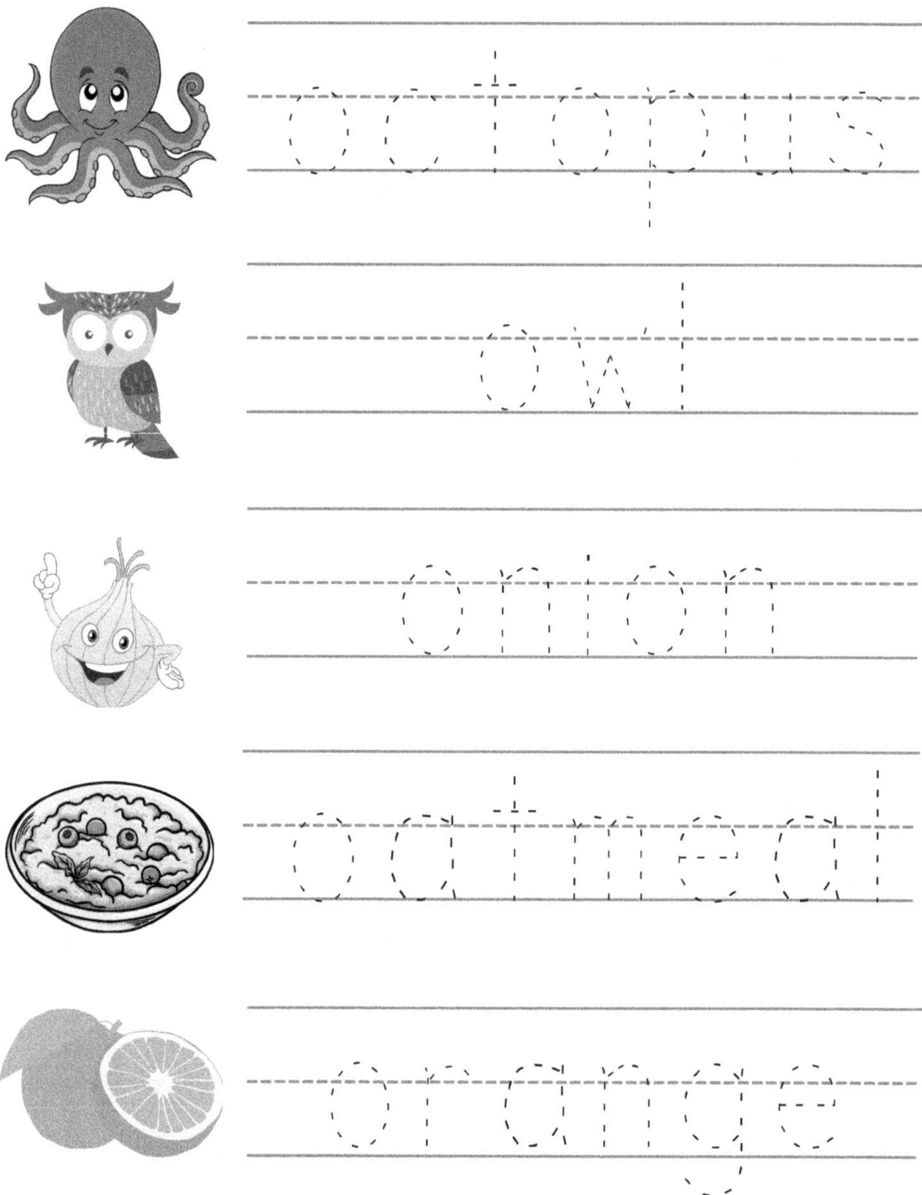

DIRECTIONS: TRACE THE WORDS THAT BEGIN WITH THE LETTER P

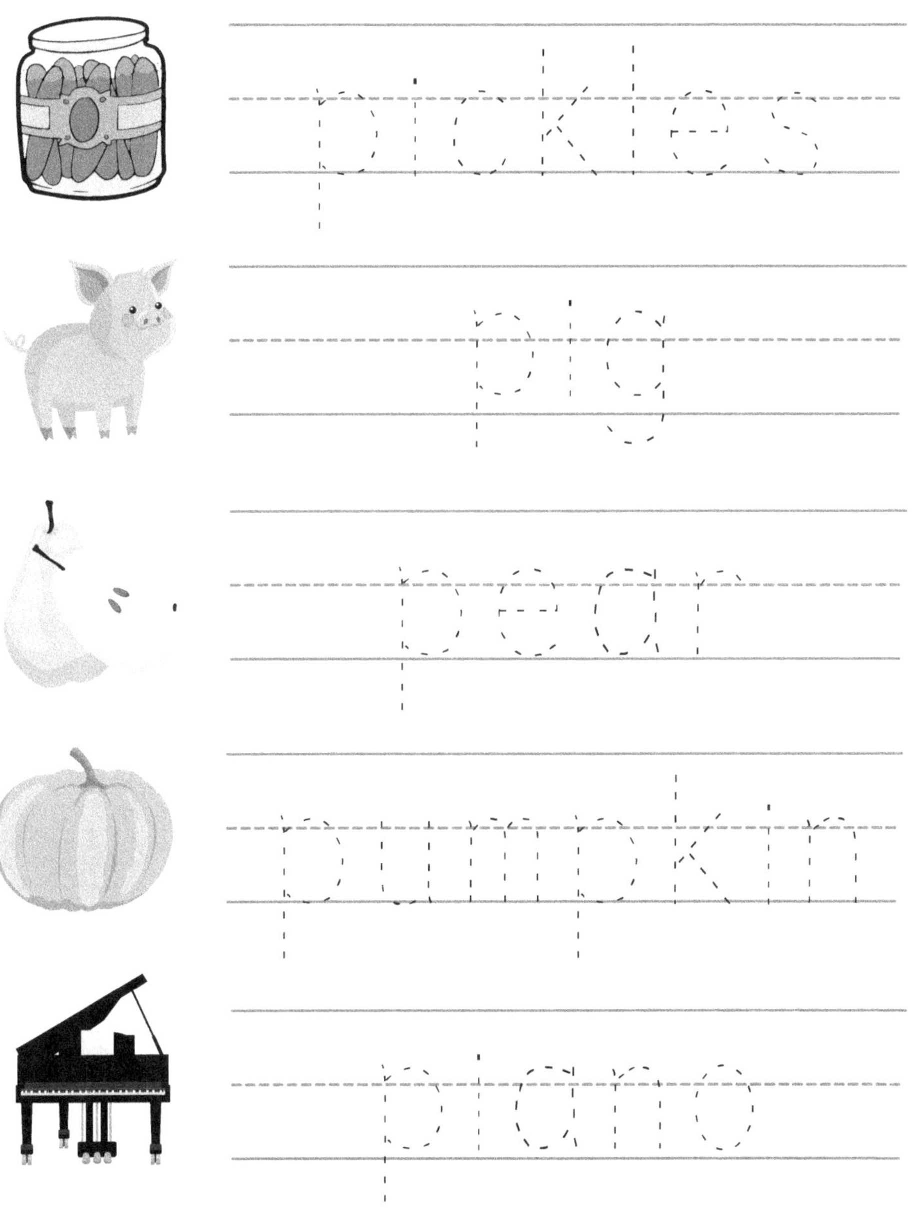

DIRECTIONS: TRACE THE WORDS THAT BEGIN WITH THE LETTER P

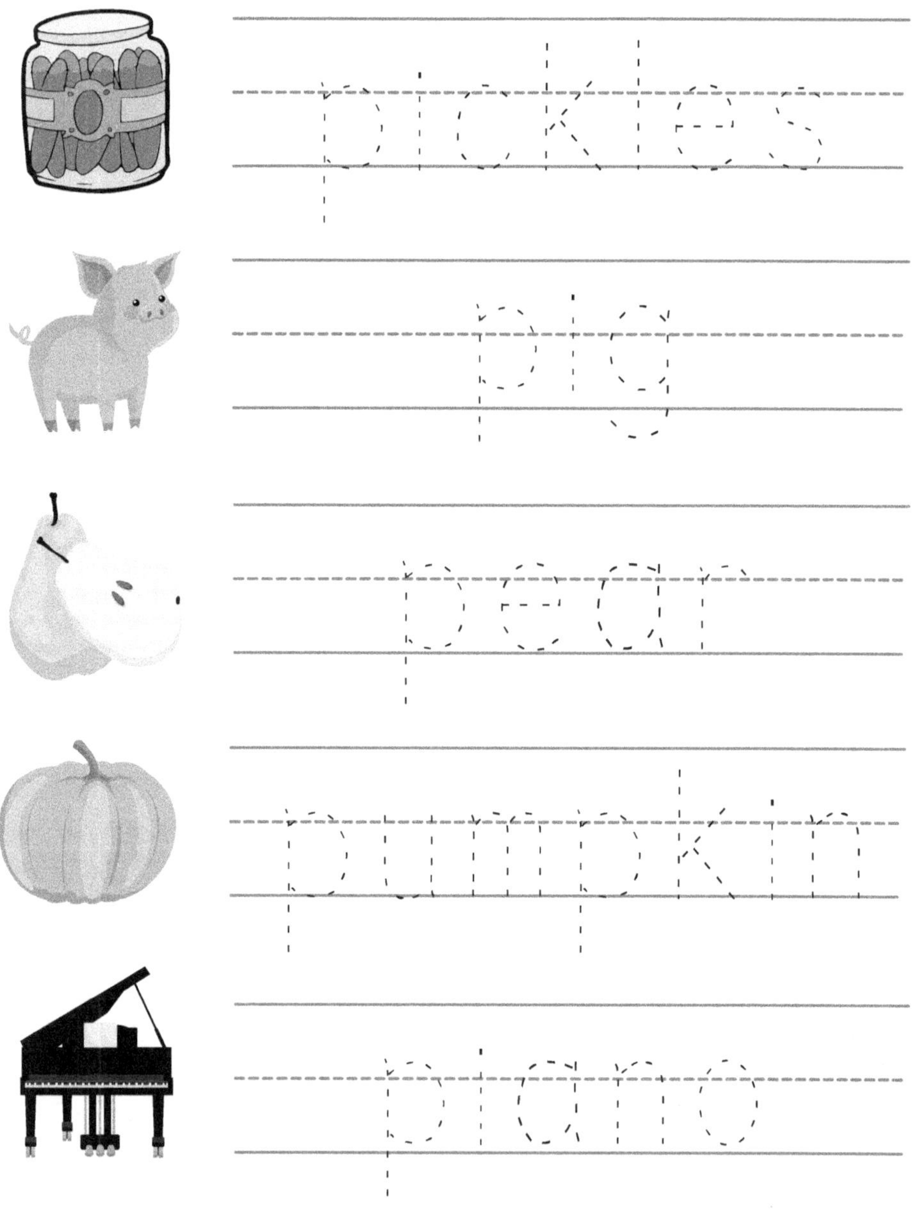

DIRECTIONS: TRACE THE WORDS THAT BEGIN WITH THE LETTER Q

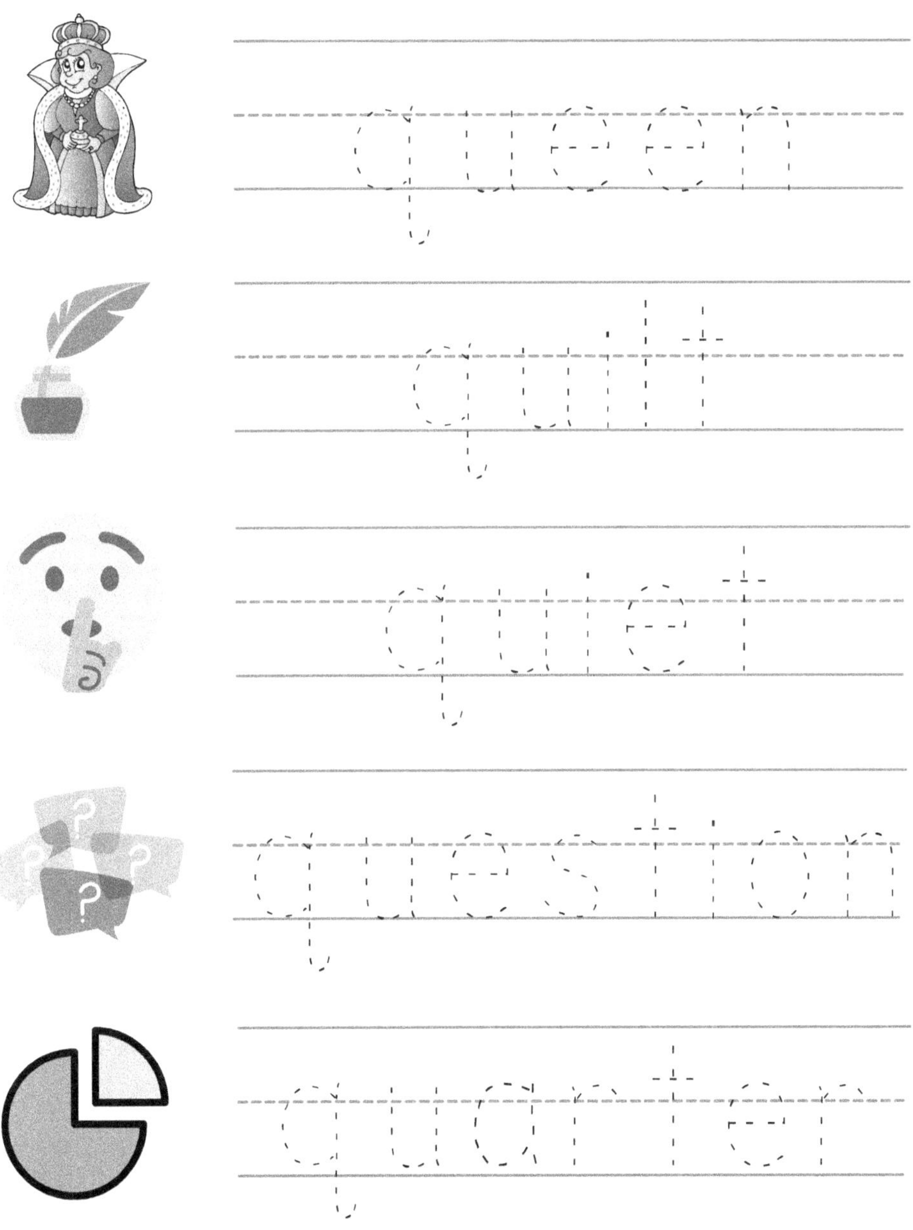

DIRECTIONS: TRACE THE WORDS THAT BEGIN WITH THE LETTER Q

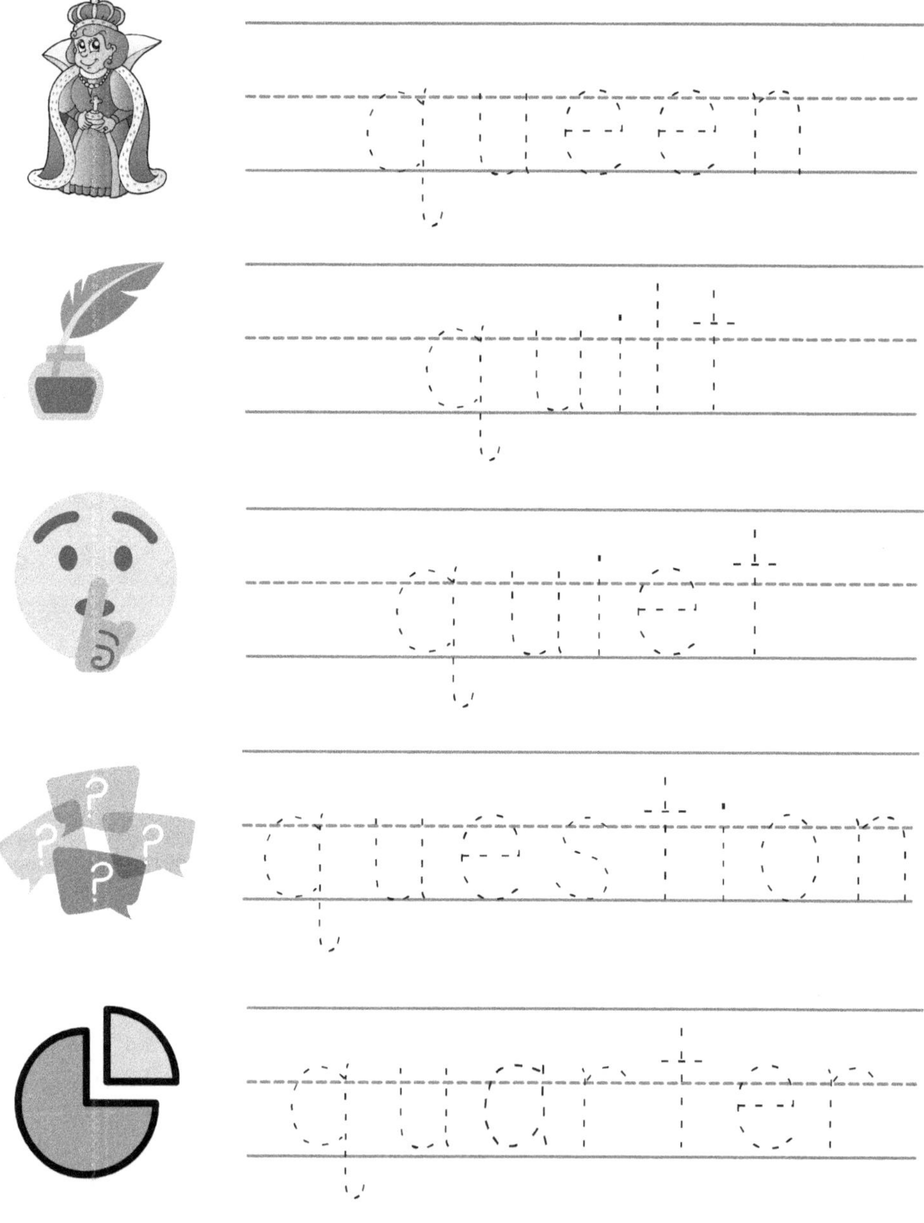

DIRECTIONS: TRACE THE WORDS THAT BEGIN WITH THE LETTER R

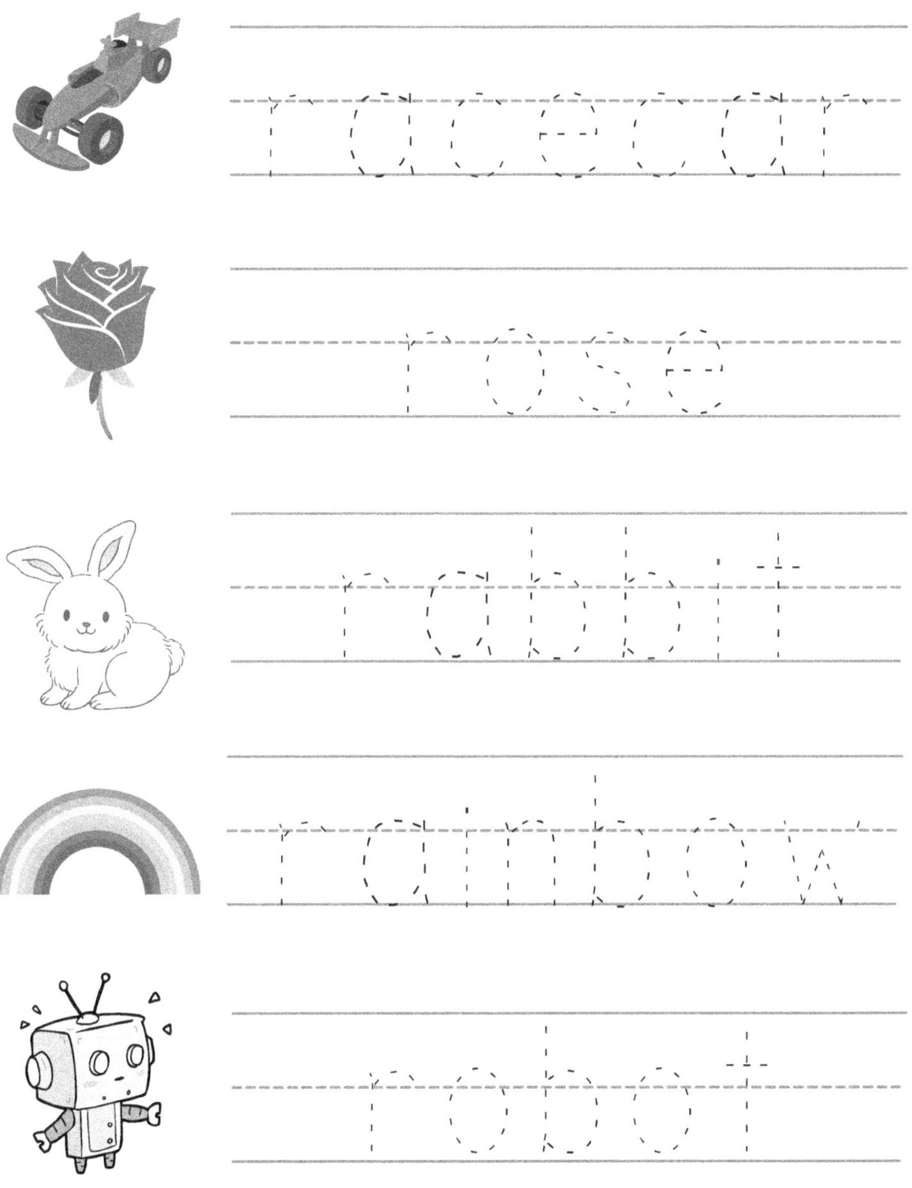

DIRECTIONS: TRACE THE WORDS THAT BEGIN WITH THE LETTER R

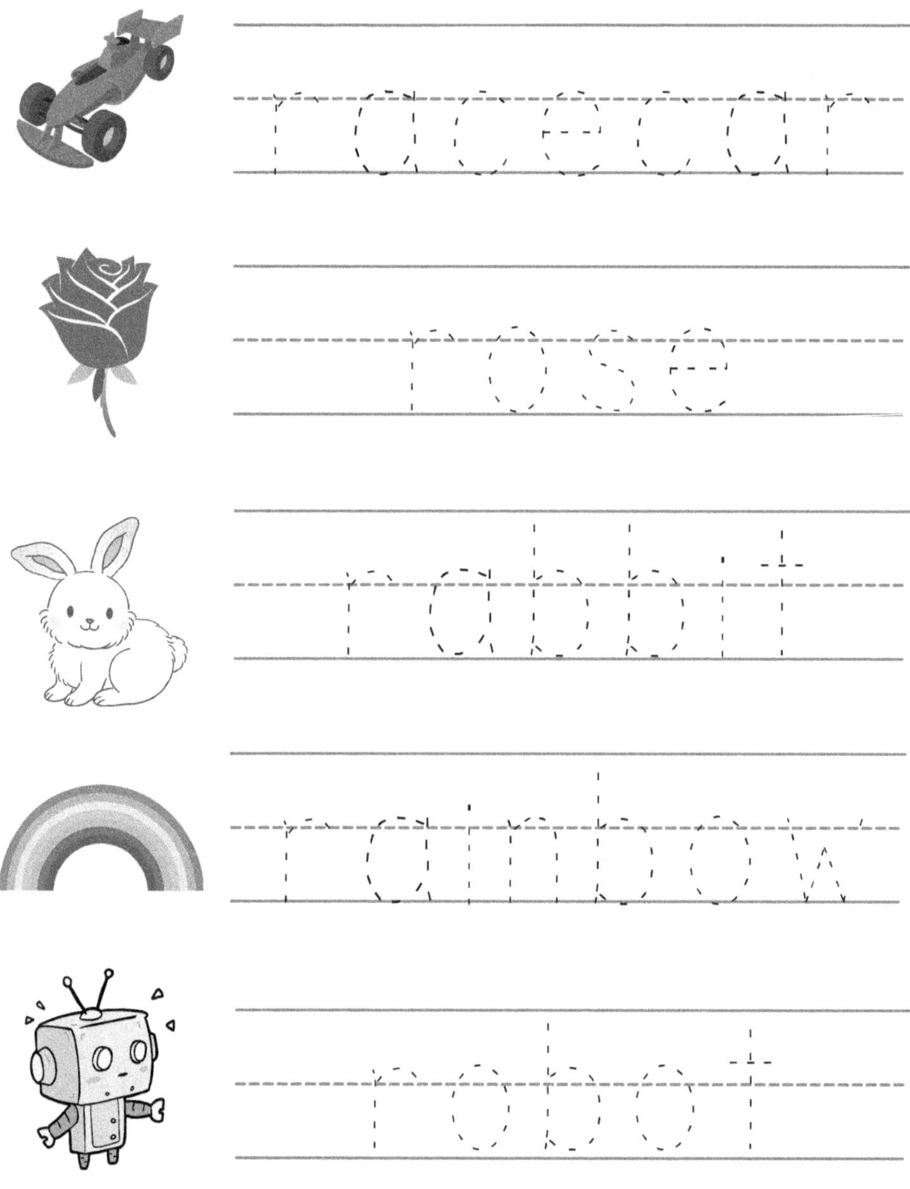

DIRECTIONS: TRACE THE WORDS THAT BEGIN WITH THE LETTER S

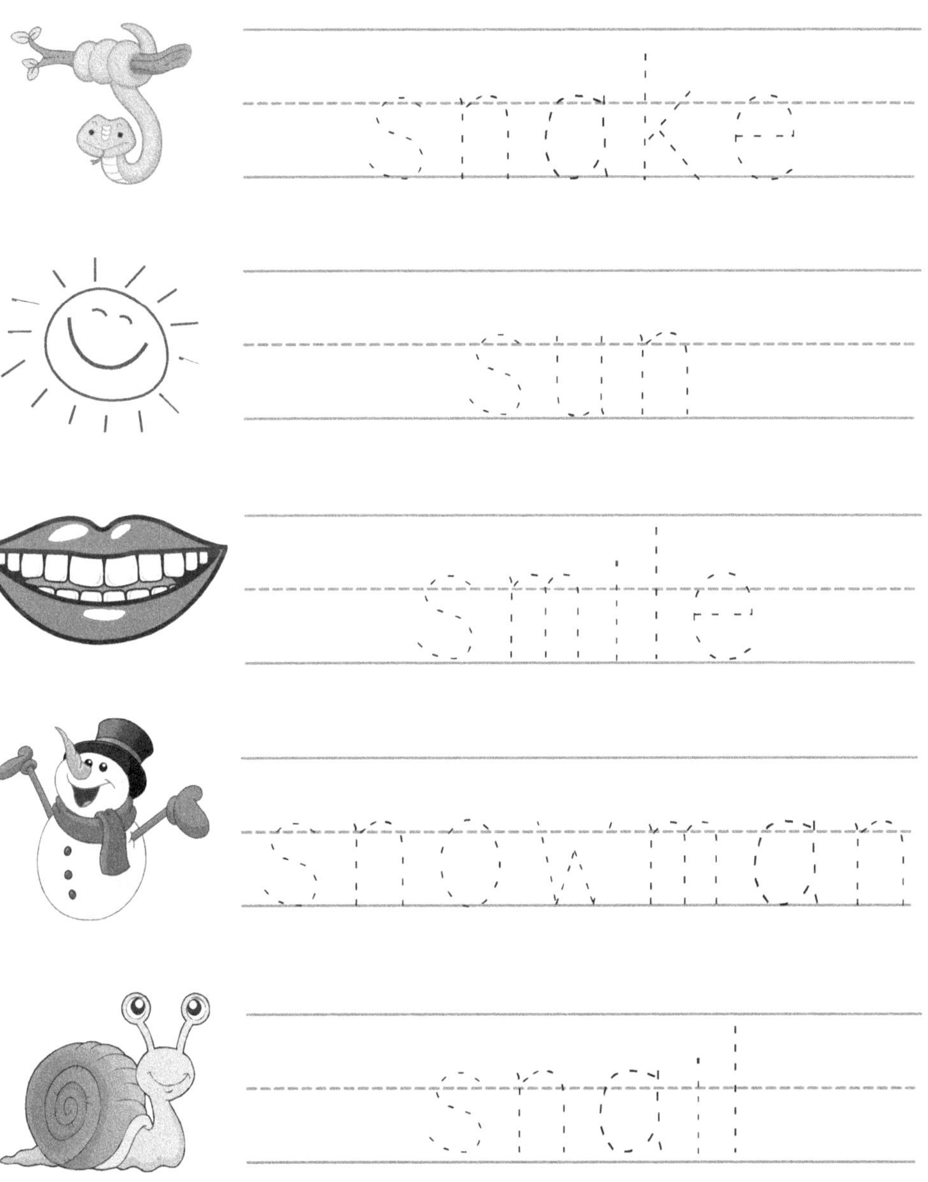

DIRECTIONS: TRACE THE WORDS THAT BEGIN WITH THE LETTER S

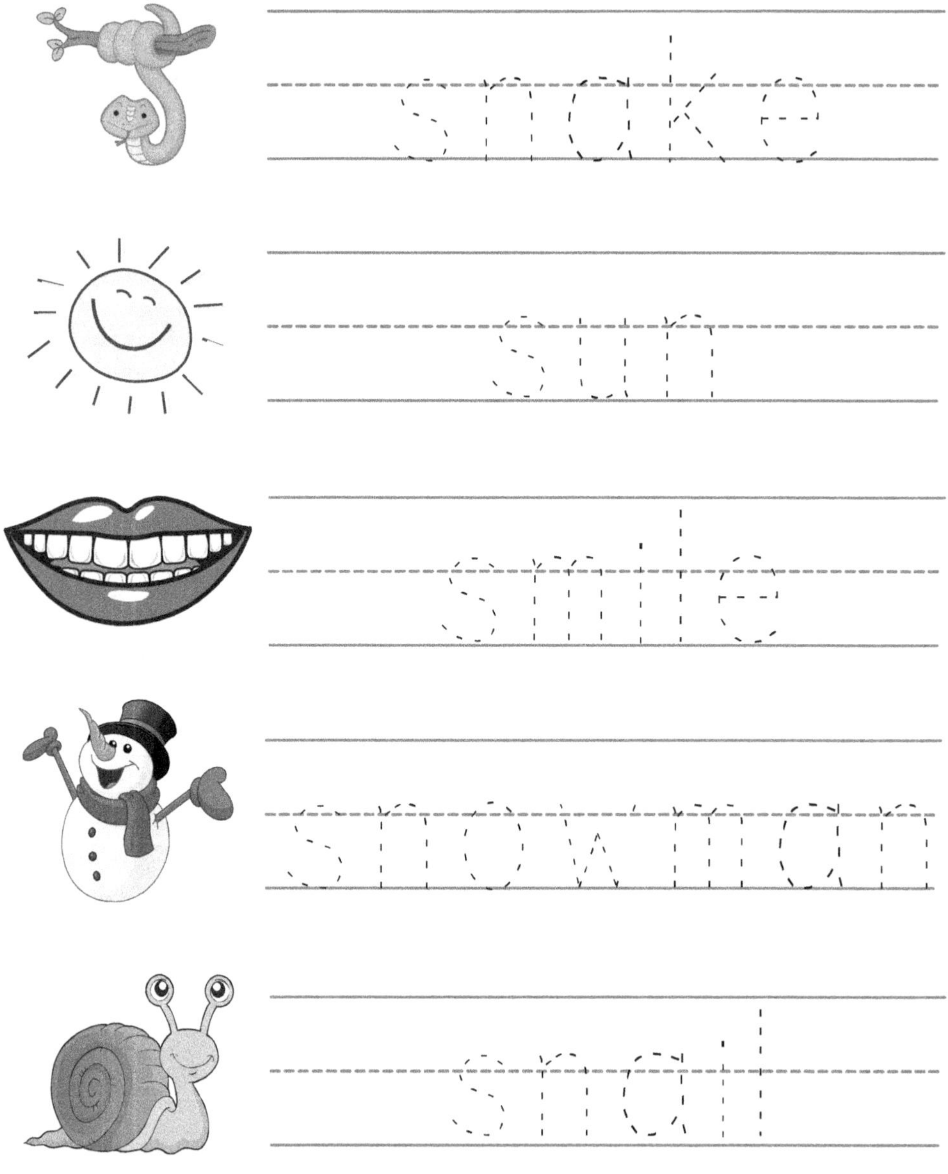

DIRECTIONS: TRACE THE WORDS THAT BEGIN WITH THE LETTER T

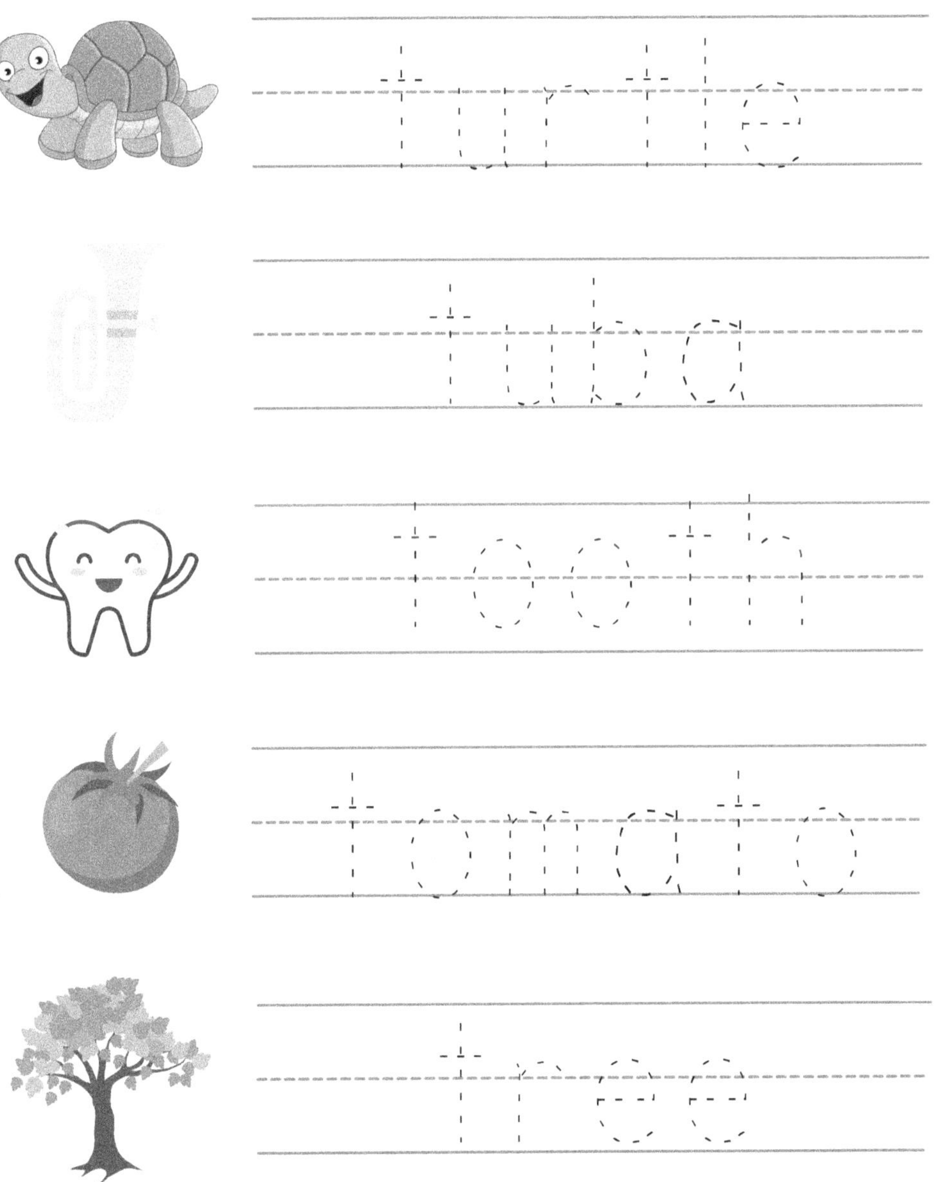

DIRECTIONS: TRACE THE WORDS THAT BEGIN WITH THE LETTER T

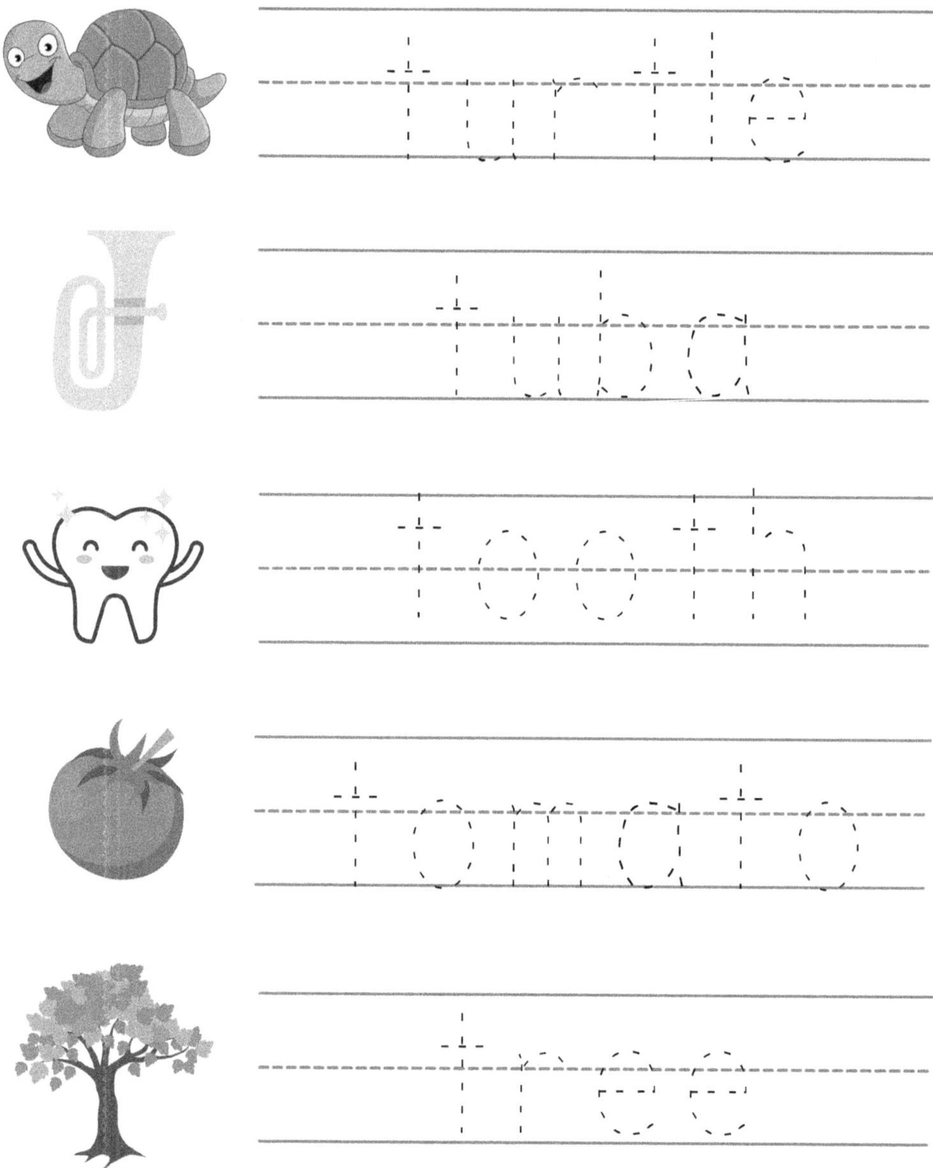

DIRECTIONS: TRACE THE WORDS THAT BEGIN WITH THE LETTER U

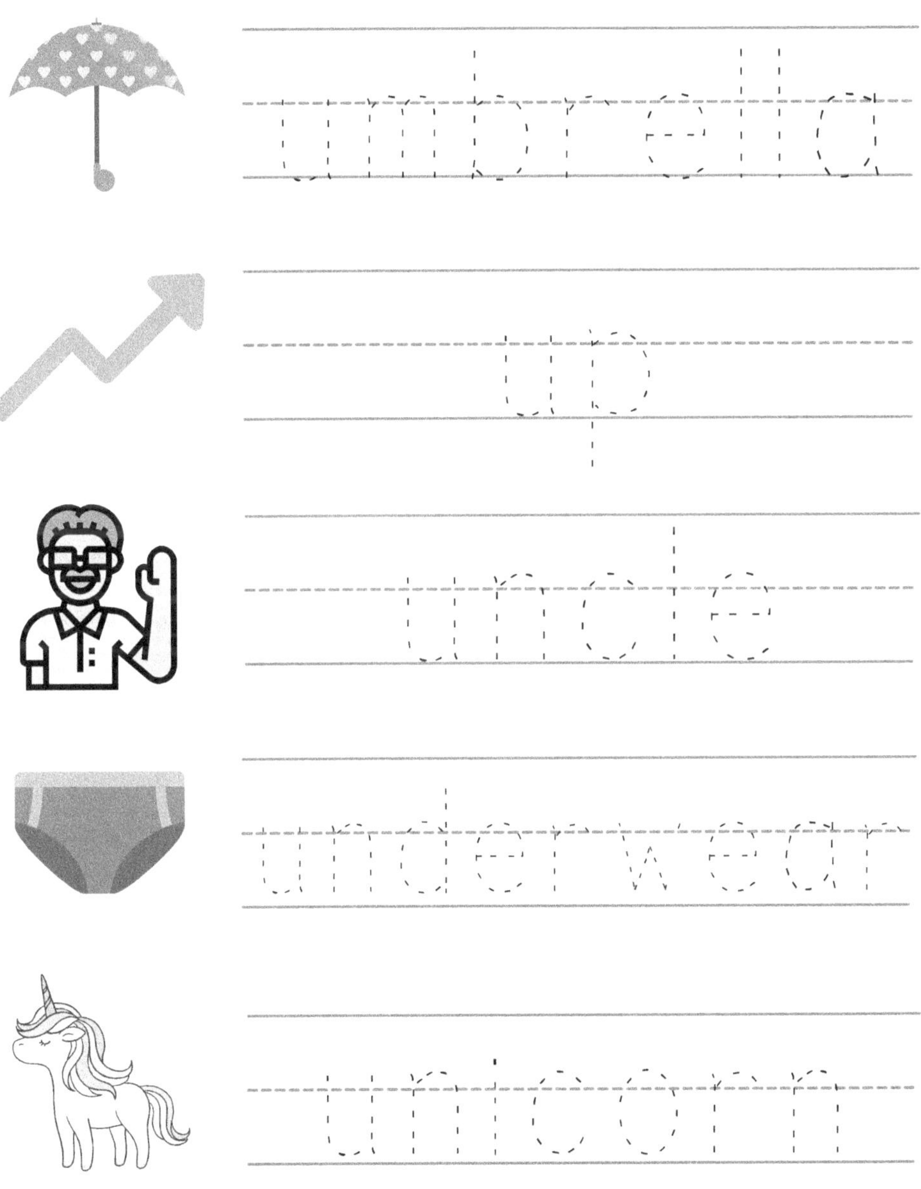

DIRECTIONS: TRACE THE WORDS THAT BEGIN WITH THE LETTER V

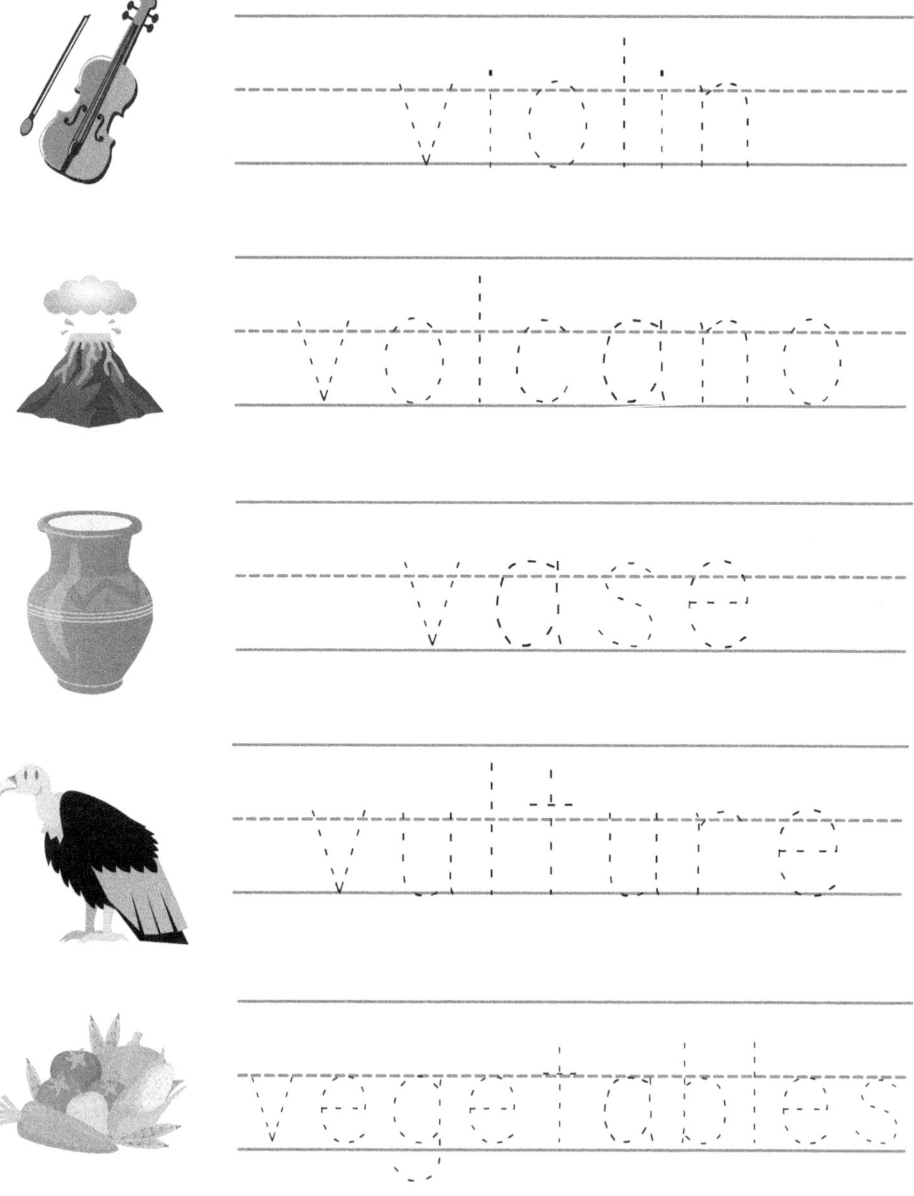

DIRECTIONS: TRACE THE WORDS THAT BEGIN WITH THE LETTER W

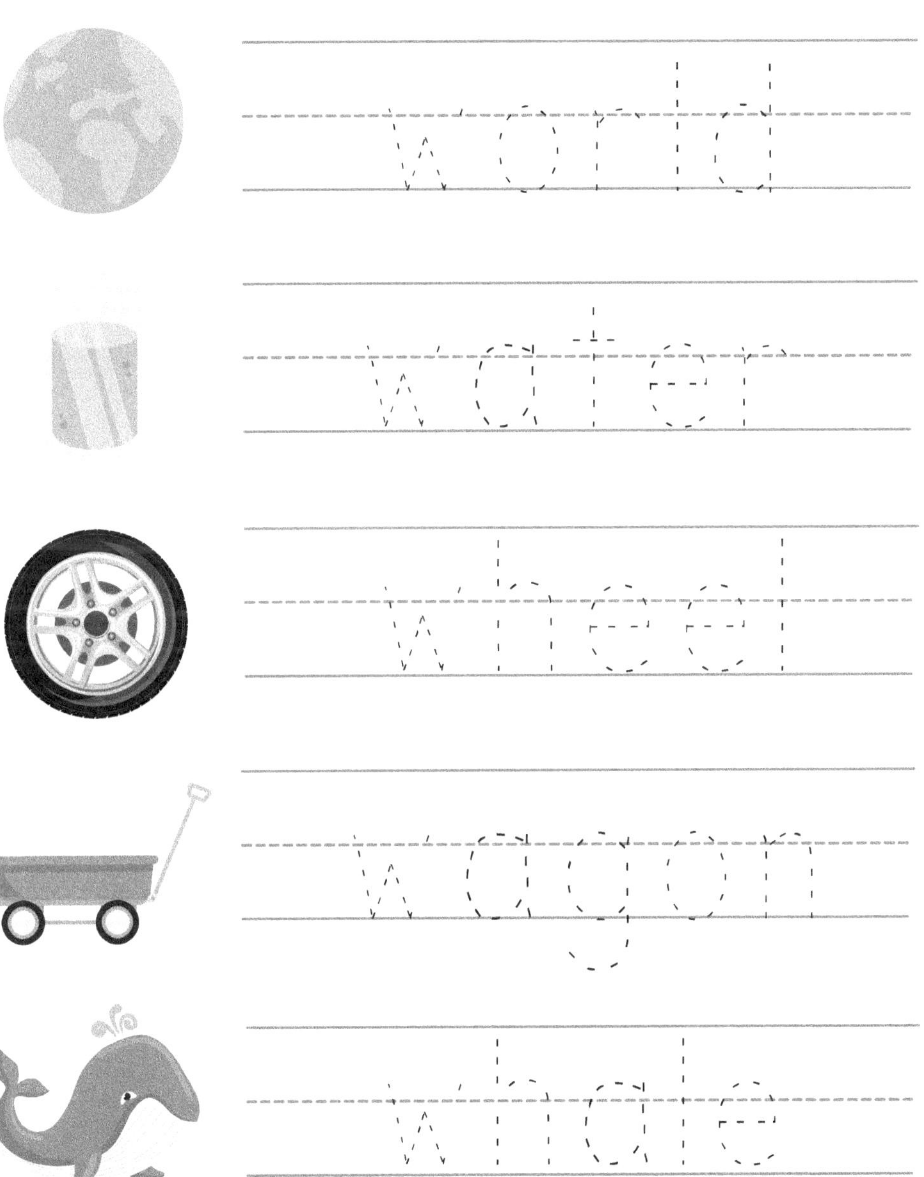

DIRECTIONS: TRACE THE WORDS THAT USE THE LETTER X

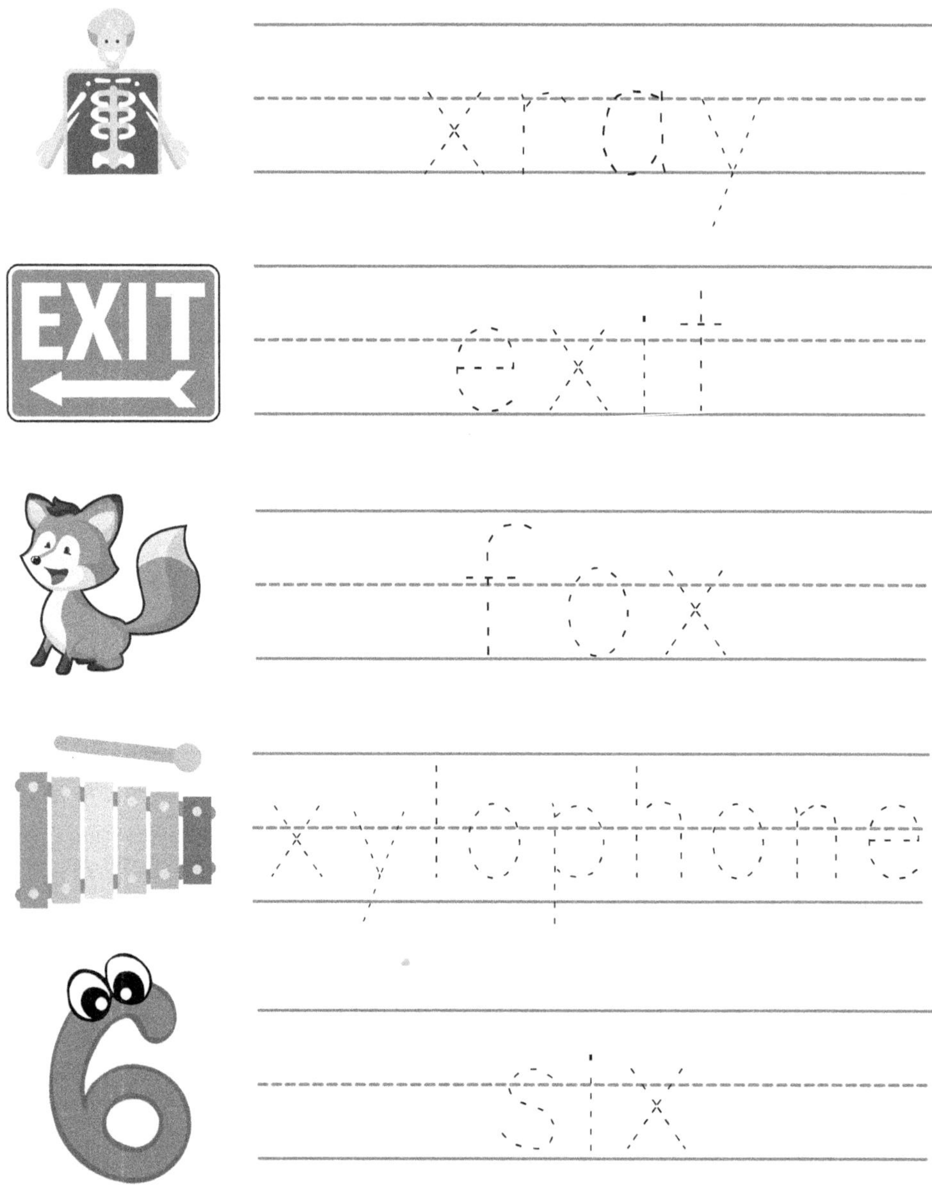

DIRECTIONS: TRACE THE WORDS THAT BEGIN WITH THE LETTER Y

DIRECTIONS: TRACE THE WORDS THAT BEGIN WITH THE LETTER Z

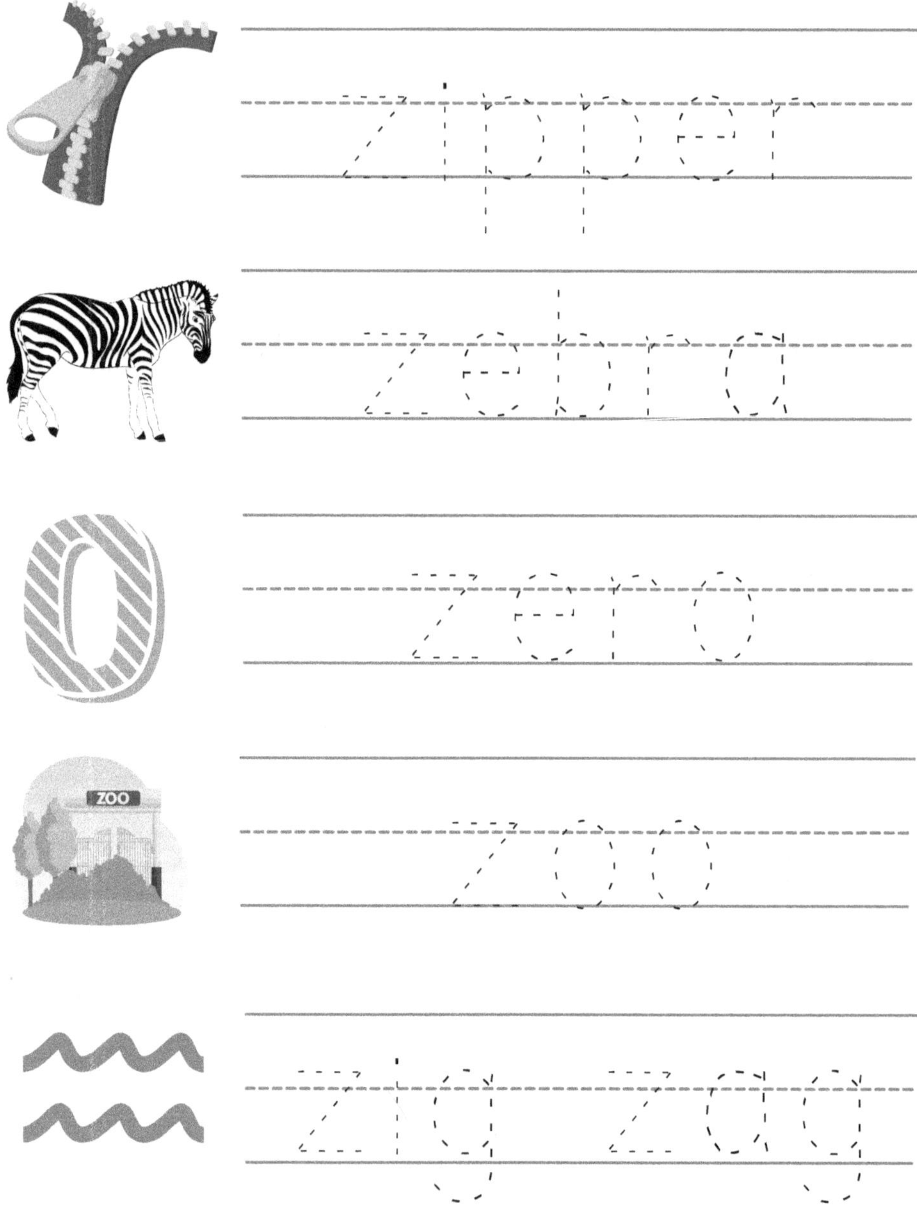

DIRECTIONS: TRACE THE WORDS THAT BEGIN WITH THE LETTER U

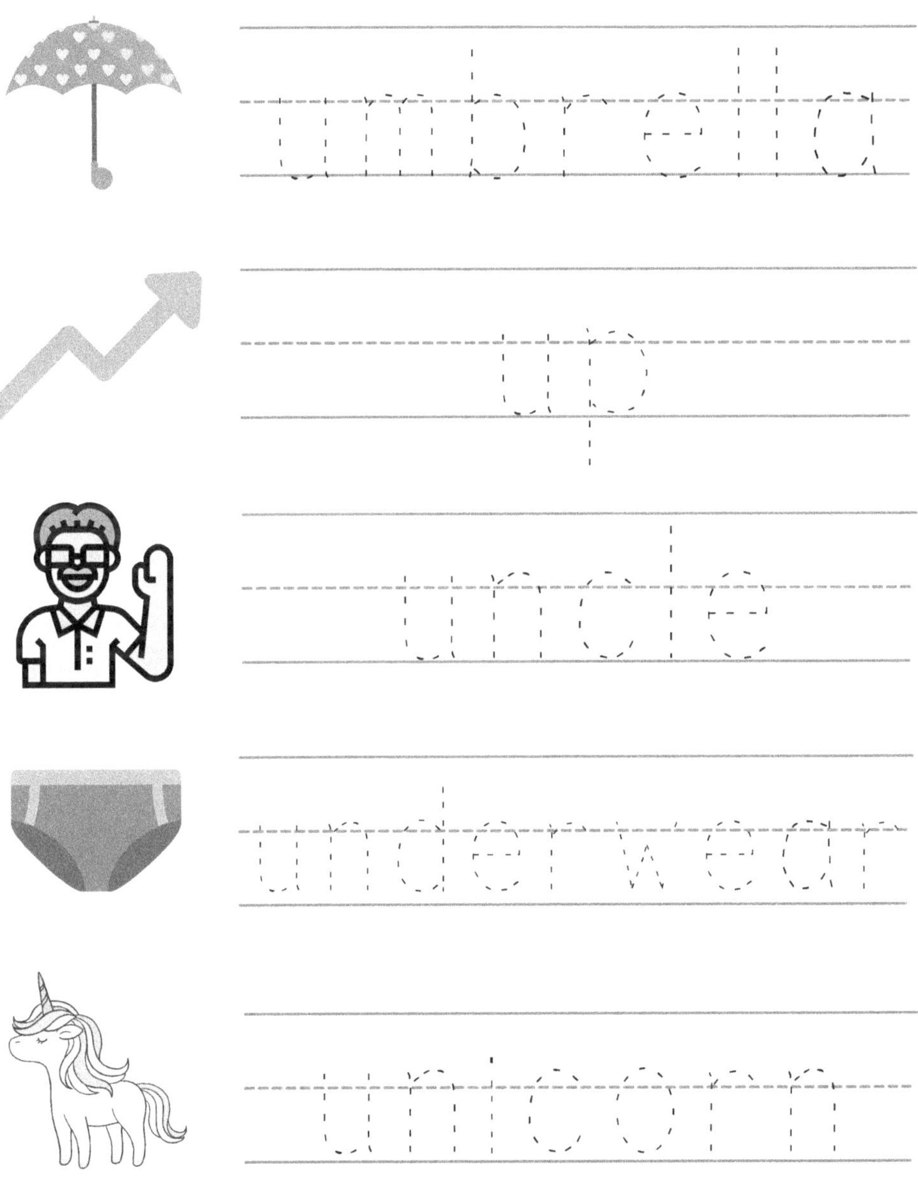

DIRECTIONS: TRACE THE WORDS THAT BEGIN WITH THE LETTER V

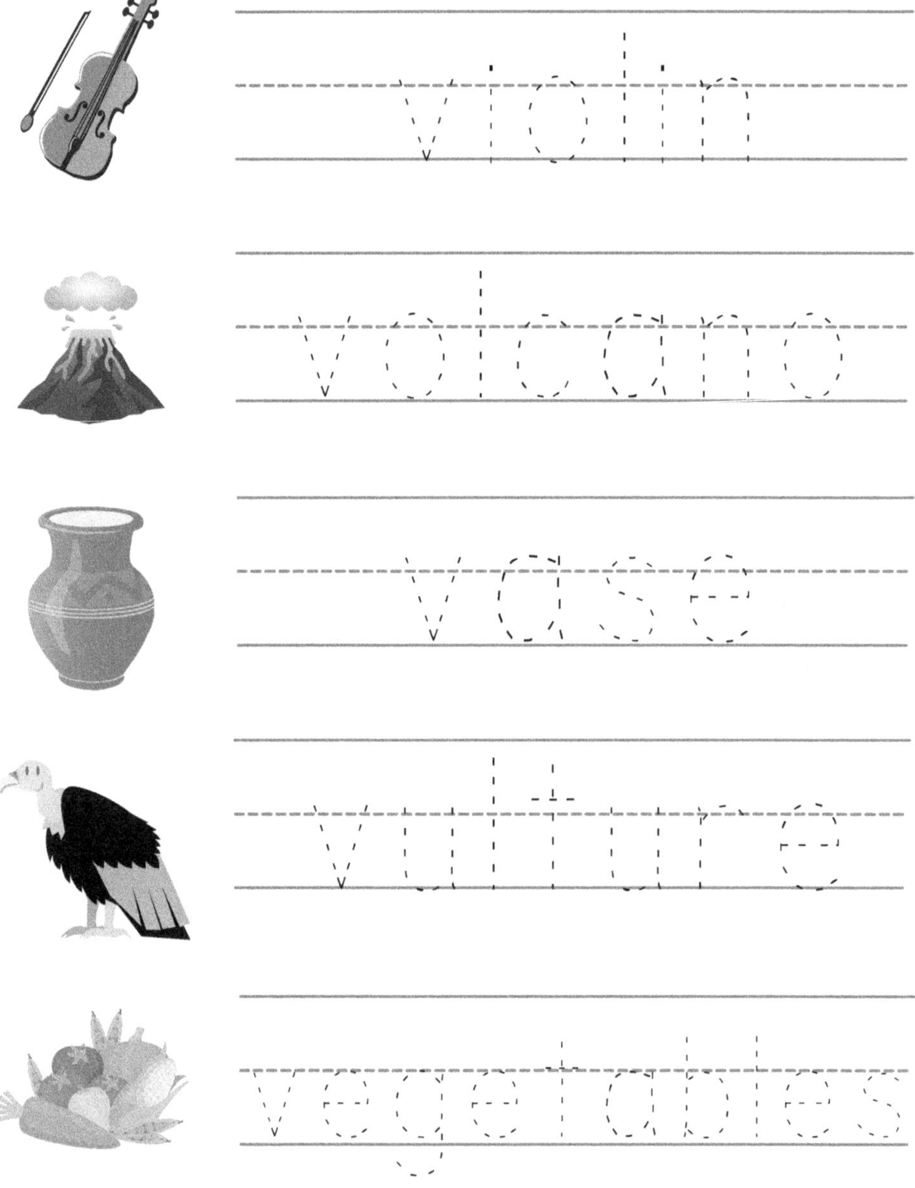

DIRECTIONS: TRACE THE WORDS THAT BEGIN WITH THE LETTER W

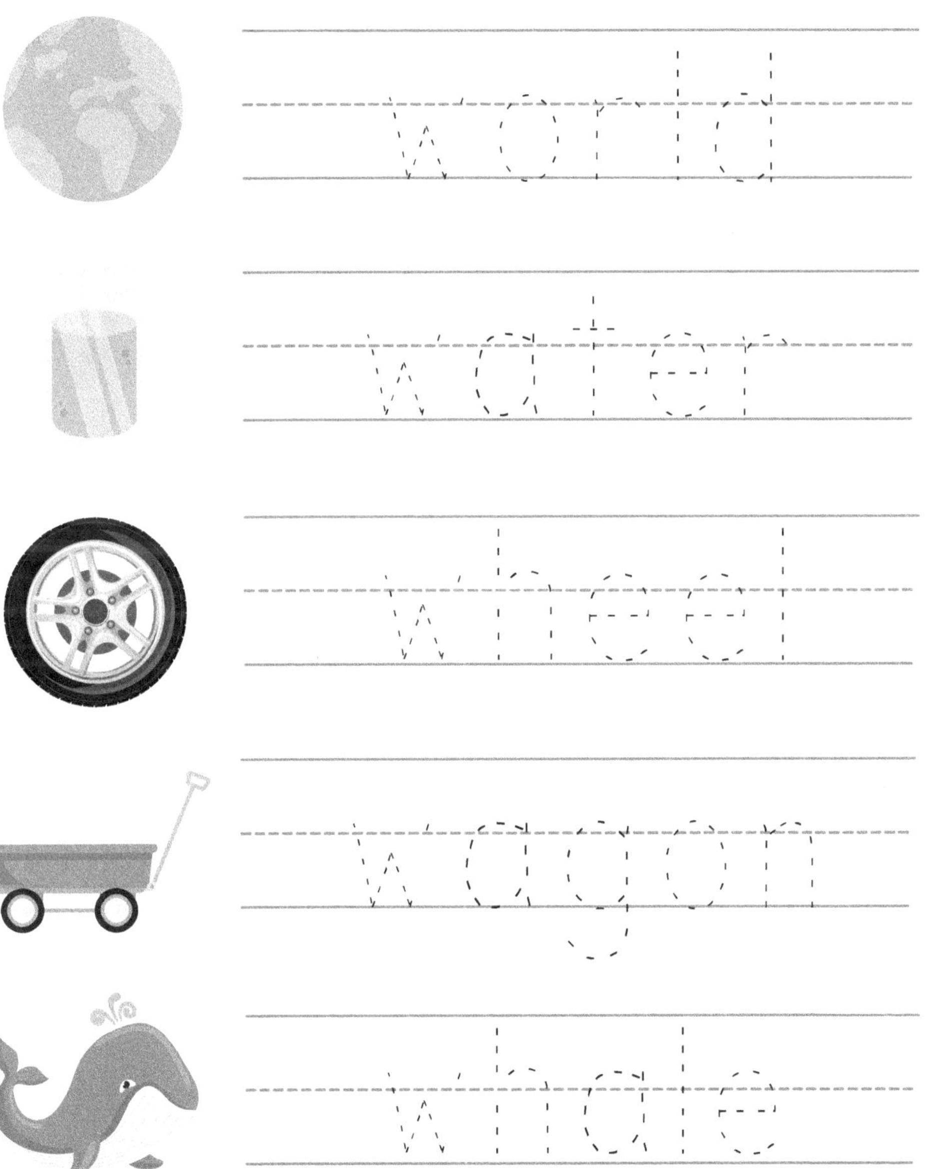

DIRECTIONS: TRACE THE WORDS THAT USE THE LETTER X

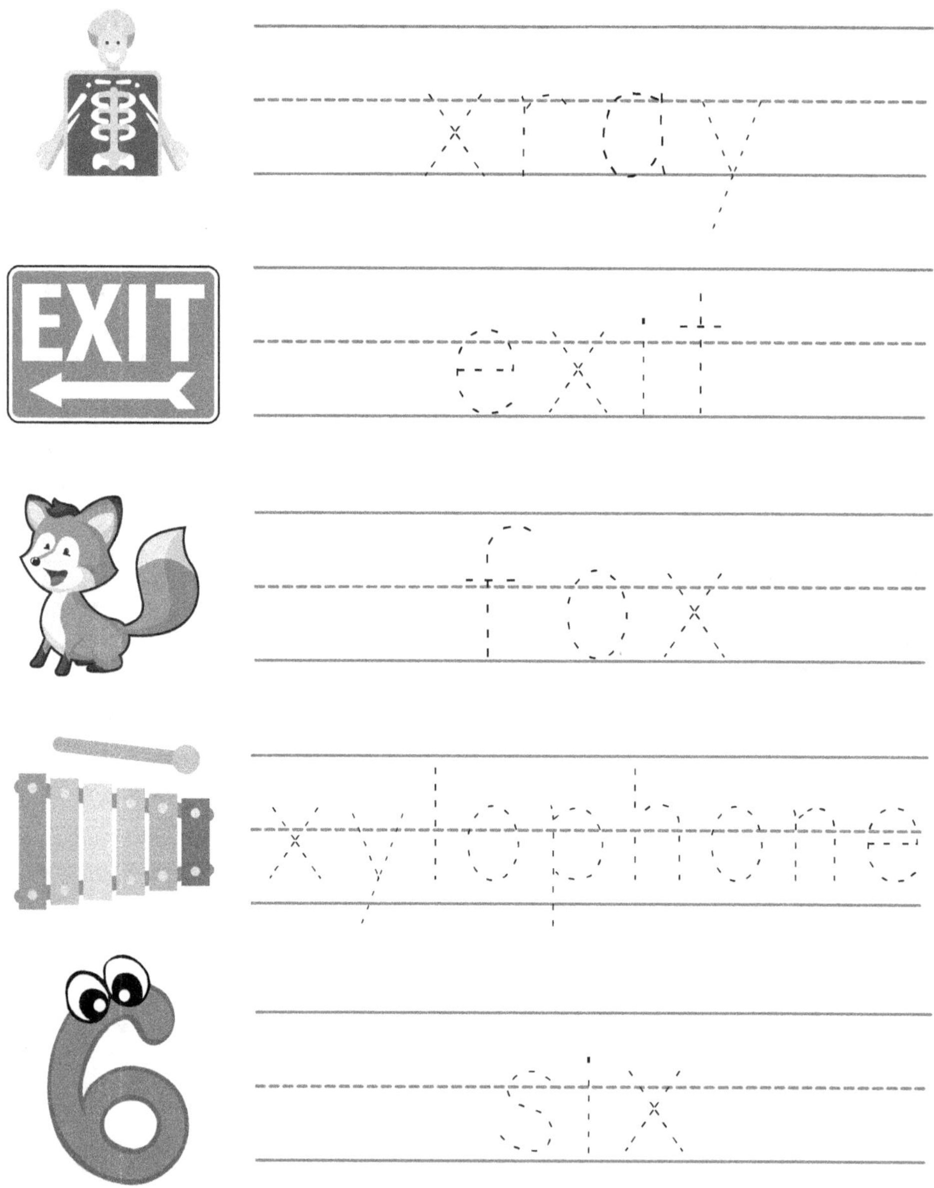

DIRECTIONS: TRACE THE WORDS THAT BEGIN WITH THE LETTER Y

DIRECTIONS: TRACE THE WORDS THAT BEGIN WITH THE LETTER Z